The John Bull

150 Years a Locomotive

John H. White, Jr.

Smithsonian Institution Press
Washington, D.C.
1981

Library of Congress Cataloging in Publication Data
White, John H.
The John Bull, 150 years a locomotive.

Bibliography: p.
1. Locomotives—History. I. Title.
TJ603.W527   625.2'61'09034   81-607054
ISBN 0-87474-961-1   AACR2

Uncredited illustrations are from the Smithsonian Institution
collections.

Cover: The *John Bull* by Elizabeth Tone Summers, 1981.

For Betsy

Contents

Acknowledgments

The National Museum of American History plans to operate the *John Bull* under its own power on the occasion of the 150th anniversary of the engine's first movement under steam, which occurred on September 15, 1831. This public demonstration will take place on the scenic Georgetown branch of the Chessie System, which follows the Chesapeake and Ohio Canal, now a national park that parallels the Potomac River. The setting is not unlike portions of the Camden and Amboy Railroad (the original owner of the engine), which followed the Delaware and Raritan Canal in New Jersey. The engine will pull a contemporaneous (ca. 1836) wooden passenger car also from the Camden and Amboy and now in the Smithsonian collections. The operating crew and passengers will be outfitted in period costume. We hope it will be a pleasant and gala celebration. Regrettably we cannot report more fully on the event because this publication must go into production nearly a year in advance in order to be ready for the celebration. It should be a notable day for all those present: they will witness the first public demonstration in fifty-four years of the world's oldest operable steam locomotive.

Many persons have helped in the testing, restoration, and promotional aspects of the celebration of the *John Bull*'s 150th year. Those inside the Smithsonian include Amy Barden, Susan Beaudette, Luis R. del Rio, Douglas Evelyn, Bernard S. Finn, Carol Hare, John Harris, Josiah Hatch, Larry Jones, Roger Kennedy, Jim Knowles, Robert C. Post, Geri Sanderson, John Stine, James McK. Symington, Robert M. Vogel, and Roger White.

Firms and individuals outside the Smithsonian that were of assistance include the Chessie System's Franklyn Carr, Milton Dolinger, John Hankey, Lloyd Lewis, C.L. Robinson, and Anthony J. Tiano; Hartford Steam Boiler Inspection and Insurance Company's Ray Badger, John Eklund, and David Spinelli; Thomas W. Sefton of the San Diego Trust and Savings Bank; James Bistline of the Southern Railway System; Herbert H. Harwood, Jr.; William D. Edson; the Cedar Run Rescue Squad; and the Catlett Volunteer Fire Company. General Telephone and Electronics provided the major funding for the September 15, celebration; a special thank you is extended to Alfred C. Viebranz of GTE. Also of assistance were George Berklacy, Mike Brown, David Sherman, and Richard Stanton of the National Park Service; Edward T. Francis; Allan Boyd and W. Graham Claytor; and William L. Withuhn.

Finally, thanks as always to my secretary, Mary E. Braunagel, who typed and proofed the manuscript.

I. The John Bull

Each year millions of visitors file past the *John Bull* locomotive where it stands, rather out of place, inside the marble-lined halls of the National Museum of American History. It is viewed by more museum patrons than any other preserved railway engine, even though it is not as historically important as Stephenson's *Rocket* or as overpowering in size as more modern locomotives. It draws this larger audience if only because of its location within the Smithsonian, now the most popular museum complex in the world. To most viewers, it is just another old train, quaint, out of date, a trifle foolish, a curiosity that is seen fleetingly as the crowds push by. To others, with a greater understanding of things historical, the *John Bull* represents a sacred relic associated with America's entry into steam railroading. Its worn, gray-black, lumpy, and well-used appearance is recognized as the patina of long service. Yet even at this level the veteran's greater significance is lost by a too limited recognition of its value as a touchstone with the past. Nostalgia makes it old, safe, and feeble. Yet it was once new, vital, and just a little frightening. In 1831 it was the most sophisticated and advanced machine of its time, analogous to a modern spaceship. Its construction and workings were understood by only a few men. It was part of a new age, the age of mechanical transport, that ended man's dependence on shoe leather and animal traction. Until the beginnings of steam railways, land transportation had changed little since Roman times. The swiftest man was astride a horse. This had been true for untold centuries. Hannibal traveled as swiftly and perhaps even a trifle more comfortably than George Washington, even though their lives were separated by nearly two millennia. And then on September 15, 1830, we suddenly have a humble North Country engineer named George Stephenson flying across the English countryside at nearly a mile a minute on the deckplate of a snorting locomotive engine. Such machines were not instantly created by divine inspiration; they were evolved rather painfully by a succession of practical mechanics who began their experiments a quarter century before Stephenson's dramatic run on the occasion of the opening of the Liverpool and Manchester Railway. The iron horse was not only swifter than its flesh-and-blood counterpart; it had greater endurance and power. It proved efficient, economical, and positively essential to the creation of heavy industry and mass public transit. The locomotive was unquestionably the stevedore for the commercial societies that arose during the nineteenth century. The major industrial nations that first appeared in Western Europe and North America were also the first to develop elaborate railway systems. Even today the underdeveloped countries have the smallest share of the world's rail mileage.

The *John Bull* was among the first of this revolutionary breed. It was built in England by Robert Stephenson, the only son of the great railway pioneer George. Robert was far and away the more gifted mechanical engineer of the pair, and the fact that he was directly involved in the design and construction of the *John Bull* adds considerably to the pedigree of the engine. It also clearly illustrates another important theme in American history: the importation of technology from Western Europe. No more direct example could be found than the *John Bull,* nor could a better demonstration be made of the ways in which a standard Old World design was modified for use in the New.

These opening remarks should alert the reader that there is more meaning to our pioneer than might be supposed at first glance. Guidebooks will tell you that it is the oldest complete and operable locomotive in the Western Hemisphere, or that it was the first engineering specimen collected by the Smithsonian. But it takes a deeper reading of the object to appreciate its worth fully. It is rather like educating a novice gallery visitor to the beauty in modern sculpture: some will never perceive it, while others will understand after sufficient study or prolonged exposure.

Autumn had come to the New York docks when Robert L. Stevens, newly appointed president and chief engineer of the Camden and Amboy Railroad, boarded the *Hibernia* bound for England.[1] Just days before he sailed on October 13, 1830, the final surveys for the railroad were completed, and it was time to procure rails and a locomotive for the new enterprise. Stevens was at once exhausted and elated. Securing the charter, raising the capital, and overseeing the novel and untried problems associated with this pioneering endeavor had made a shambles of the last two years. The six-week sea journey would be a welcome respite from these cares. Stevens was not, however, a man to languish or waste time, and he soon began to think about the right style of rail for the Camden line. Thought led to action. A penknife and a block of pine ultimately produced a model of what was to become the standard pattern of railroad rail used throughout the world. During the long hours of his Atlantic crossing, Stevens conjured the basic design for the T-rail, one of the most rational structural shapes ever devised. This incident has been referred to frequently in the annals of American railroad history, and yet one wonders what thought, if any, Stevens gave to the new

Figure 1. The *John Bull* appears today as modified in 1876 for exhibit at the United States Centennial in Philadelphia. *(Scientific American Supplement,* June 9, 1900.)

locomotives.

That Stevens set out for England with any definite pre-conceptions seems unlikely, for he had never seen an actual working locomotive. Yet he was hardly an innocent about steam engines. He had been directly involved in the construction and design of several steamers and was unquestionably familiar with a steam wagon built for the circular railway in his father's amusement park in 1825.[2] This small experimental machine was not, and was never intended to be, a practical motive power unit for a commercial railway. It was little more than an oversized toy meant to demonstrate steam power. In neither its general arrangement nor in any of its details did it influence future locomotive design. If his father's experiment was of limited use, where else might Stevens have gained some knowledge of locomotive design? There was almost no opportunity to have done so in North America. The few texts on the subject, such as William Strickland's report published in 1826, discussed only obsolete, slow-moving, colliery-type engines that would hardly have suited the needs of a public railway intended for relatively fast passenger trains. He might have visited the West Point Foundry to observe the progress being made on a new engine for the South Carolina Railroad. This machine shop was not too far from the dock where Steven's steamboats landed in lower Manhattan. Anyone with an engineering interest would have been drawn by the novelty of such a new endeavor: the *Best Friend* was, after all, the first locomotive built for commercial service in this country. Even if Stevens went to see the *Best Friend,* he wisely decided not to copy it. It embodied a plan that was not duplicated.[3] There was little opportunity for Stevens to study locomotive design in this country in

1830, although numerous false starts were being made at about this time, by native mechanics who felt originality rather than rational planning was the key to good design. The curious schemes of America's pioneer locomotive designers, such as Stephen H. Long, William T. James, and William Howard, led nowhere. More practical mechanics realized that it was more prudent to study the work of those already experienced in locomotive construction and then modify their plans for American needs. In 1830 there was only one place to observe established railway engine builders, and that was England.

Once ashore it must not have taken Stevens long to realize that the British, particularly Robert Stephenson, were decades ahead of anyone else in the field of railway engineering.[4] The members of this ferruginous race were simply masters in ironworking and machinery fabrication. They had been the leading technologists since 1712, when Thomas Newcomen (1663–1729) produced the first steam-pumping engine for draining tin and coal mines. Newcomen's ponderous atmospheric engine was refined and greatly improved by Watt and other skillful mechanics during the mid- and late-1700s, when it was adopted for factories, steamboats, and, in time, railway locomotion. It was in 1804 that steam was first harnessed for railway use by Richard Trevithick, a Cornish mechanic who adapted one of his high-pressure portable engines for the purpose. By the final years of the Napoleonic era, crude, slow-moving locomotives were operating on a few coal-hauling railroads in the north of England. These squat, ungainly boilers-on-wheels, bristling with rivets, exposed gears, and walking beams, would hardly suggest to most observers that steam would ever evolve into anything that was fleet or streamlined. However, the evolution was relatively rapid and was much like the hideous caterpillar's transformation into an elegant butterfly. Many minds contributed to this revolution in locomotive design that indeed took place in the truly revolutionary period of about five months. The best minds of the era combined to produce the first modern locomotive, the Liverpool and Manchester Railway's *Rocket*. It broke away from the established colliery-style engine. Gone were single-flue boilers, gears, and walking beams. They were replaced by a multitubular boiler and a direct, gearless drive. Complexity was replaced by simplicity. The *Rocket* was capable of fast steaming and fast running. She was light, nicely proportioned, and neatly fitted up. She set the basic pattern for all subsequent main-line steam locomotives.

No one man can claim credit for all of the good ideas embodied in the *Rocket*, but if anyone can be singled out for the major credit, that person is Robert Stephenson. He had literally been raised in the shadow of locomotives—his father, George, the illustrious engineer and railway builder, was an unknown engine-wright employed by a coal mine near Newcastle, England, when Robert was a lad. The father's work in the repair of hoisting and pumping engines led him to experiment with self-propelling steam engines. The results of his efforts were not remarkable, but he built a number of workable machines and slowly developed a reputation for railway building. As his civil-engineering career progressed, he had less time for locomotives. He foresaw a growing market for such machines and so in 1823 helped to organize, in Newcastle, the firm of Robert Stephenson and Company. His son, just nineteen years of age, was put in charge of the firm named in his honor. It was the first manufacturing establishment created especially for the construction of railway engines. Specialization and the concentration of effort resulted in leadership in this new and narrow field. In a very few years this young man, born in a rented room of a Tyneside cottage, became the world's foremost expert on locomotive construction and design. And so it was to this man that Robert Stevens turned for counsel on the purchase of a locomotive for his projected railway in faraway New Jersey.

Just nine days before Stevens sailed for England, Stephenson delivered a new locomotive, the *Planet,* to the Liverpool and Manchester Railway. It incorporated several improvements over the *Rocket* and its sisters and illustrates the rapid progress that often occurs during the first years of a new technology. The boiler was similar to the *Rocket's,* but the firebox was fully incorporated inside the boiler proper, a step that not only cleaned up the design but promoted greater thermal efficiency. Conversely the smokebox was fully developed as a separate unit on the front of the boiler, creating an enclosed space for the blast-pipes, the dry- or steam-delivery pipes, a base for the smokestack, and, of course, a chamber for the unburned products of combustion to gather before they were exhausted out of the stack. The cylinders were placed inside the frames in the lower portion of the smokebox. In this well-insulated situation, thermal efficiency was again increased. And because the cylinders were placed so near the center of the locomotive, the oscillation of the engine, caused by the reciprocating parts of the engine, was somewhat dampened (fig. 2). The power was transported via a crank axle on the rear set of wheels rather than by pin cranks formed on the driving wheels of an outside con-

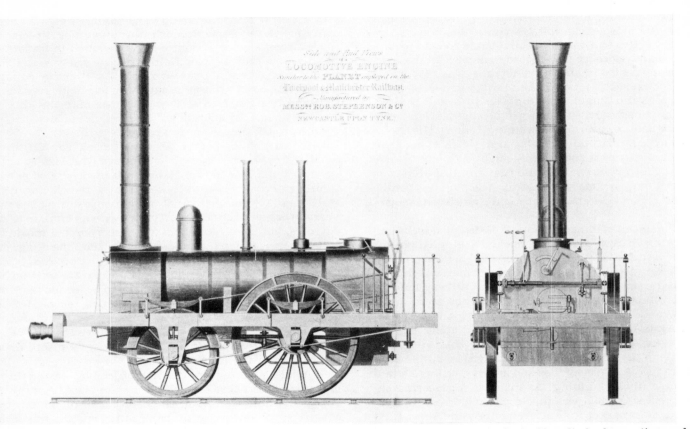

Figure 2. The *Planet*-style engine introduced in 1830 by Robert Stephenson set the basic pattern for inside-cylinder locomotives so long favored in Great Britain. The *John Bull* was made by the same maker and incorporated many of the design elements shown in this drawing. (Courtesy of the Science Museum, London.)

Figure 3. Edward Bury's *Liverpool* was undergoing tests at the time of Robert Stevens's English tour. It also influenced the final design of the *John Bull*. (Courtesy of the Science Museum, London.)

nected engine. The general arrangement described here became immensely popular in Great Britain and persisted into the twentieth century. When first introduced it was seen as the best plan available. Stevens reportedly saw the *Planet* in service before proceeding to Newcastle. And so, to one whose head was clear of any preconceived ideas of just what a proper locomotive should look like, the *Planet* seemed the perfect engine.

But not quite perfect; for by the time Stevens drafted specifications with Stephenson, dated December 6, 1830 (*see* Appendix B), he had some notions of his own. He was not ready to order a mere duplicate of the *Planet*. In fact he preferred the *Planet*'s big brother, the *Samson*, for his pattern. The latter was a larger version of the original plan intended to push heavy trains up long grades. All four wheels were of the same size and all were powered through the medium of four outside cranks and a pair of connecting rods. But he was not ready to order a stock "four coupled *Planet*," as the *Samson* class was known. He wanted a light engine more on the scale of the *Planet*, with smaller cylinders and boiler rather than the standard *Samson* class. He also came to admire the dome firebox introduced by one of Stephenson's rivals, Edward Bury of Liverpool. Bury was testing an engine on the Liverpool and Manchester line at the time of Steven's visit (fig. 3). Named in honor of his home town, Bury's machine was in many ways a smaller version of the *Samson*. Some critics have even claimed that Stephenson copied the *Liverpool*—a dispute mentioned but never fully resolved by British locomotive historians.[5] Whatever the merits of this allegation, Stevens was impressed by the domed firebox, and in his December 1830 memorandum agreement with Stephenson he called for the

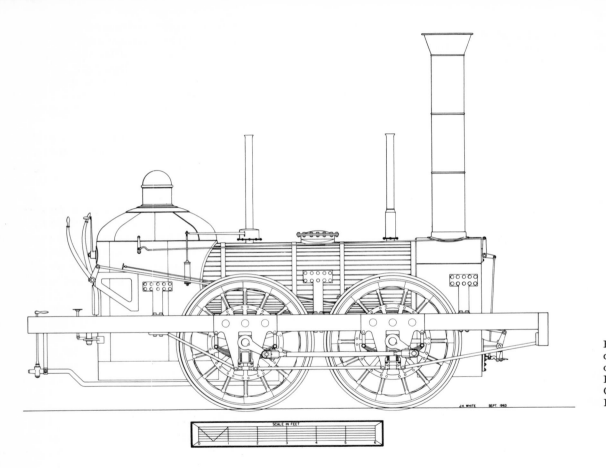

SCALE IN FEET

Figure 4. A reconstruction drawing of the *John Bull* as originally built in 1831 by Robert Stephenson and Company. (Drawing by John H. White, Jr.)

firebox to be made as a vertical cylinder. He did not in fact exactly copy Bury's design, for in the plan view Stevens's firebox was circular (fig. 5) while Bury's was D-shaped. The scheme was not even fully developed. The *Liverpool* had a low, flattish profile, while the fully developed Bury firebox was crowned by a hemispherical top that provided generous steam room, the one great advantage of this plan. Actually the design, even in its maturity, had more faults than advantages—it was expensive and difficult to fabricate and offered only a limited grate area. As first offered by Bury and as copied by Stevens for the *John Bull,* it lacked the big steam space that might have justified this costly alternative to Stephenson's simpler wagon-top firebox with its rectangular grate.

Except for the shape of the firebox, the purchaser prudently allowed the maker to execute the remaining details of the engine on his own proven plan. Stevens did ask that Jones's wheels be used " . . . if not found objectionable . . . "; however, there appears to have been some objection, and Stephenson supplied wooden wheels braced with wrought-iron crank rings (figs. 4 and 8).[6]

Only fragmentary evidence exists on the *John Bull* as first built. A contemporary order book provides a description of "Mr. Stephen's [*sic*] locomotive constructed June 1831" (*see* p. 20. It might be noted that in none of the contemporary records of the Stephenson Company is the engine referred to as the *John Bull.* This name was apparently not applied until some time after the engine entered service and may not have been used until after the machine reached the relic stage of its career.)[7]

There is in addition to this table of dimensions a contemporary drawing of the boiler (fig. 6). This drawing and the

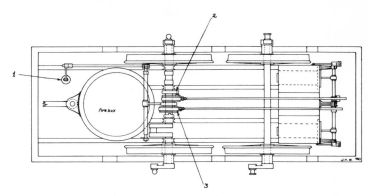

Figure 5. A plan view of the *John Bull*'s original running gear: *1* is the foot-treadle reverse, *2* is the gab, and *3* is one of the eccentrics.

		ft.	in.
BOILER	Diameter	2	6
	Length	6	9
SMOKE BOX	Length	2	2
	Breadth	4	1
	Depth below Boiler	2	-
FIRE BOX	Outside Diameter	4	1
	Depth below boiler	1	4
	Total Height	5	3¼
	Inside Diameter	3	7
FIRE GRATE	Area of Fire Grate	10.07 sq. ft.	
CHIMNEY	Diameter		13½
	Area	143 sq. ins.	
NO. OF TUBES		82	
	Diameter		1⅝
	Area	145 sq. in.	
HEATING SURFACE	Heating surface of tubes	261.7 sq. ft.	
	” ” ” Fire Box	34.8 ” ”	
		296.5 ” ”	
CYLINDERS	Diameter	9	
	Stroke	20	
DOUBLE SLIDE VALVES			
WHEELS (COUPLED)	Diameter	4	6
	Centres	4	11
FRAME	Length	14	9
	Width	6	3
WOOD INSIDE FRAMES			

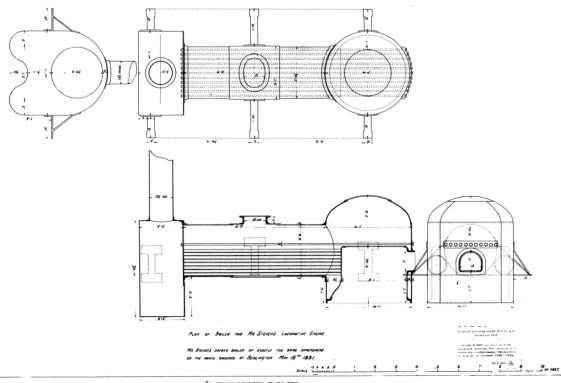

PLAN OF BOILER FOR MR STEVENS LOCOMOTIVE ENGINE.

MR STEVENS SECOND BOILER OF EXACTLY THE SAME DIMENSIONS
AS THE ABOVE ORDERED BY BEDLINGTON MAY 18TH 1831.

SCALE

THE DRAWING IS ENDORSED ON THE BACK
"STEVENS LOCOMOTIVE"
"PLAN OF STEAM BOILER"

TRACED FROM AN ORIGINAL DRAWING IN THE POSSESSION OF ROBERT STEPHENSON & Co

Figure 6. A tracing of
the original drawing
used for the *John Bull's*
boiler. (Courtesy of
English Electric.)

specifications, together with the many contemporary sketches and drawings reproduced in Warren's centennial history of Robert Stephenson and Company, were combined to produce a side elevation of the *John Bull* as it appeared at the time of its completion on June 18, 1831 (fig. 4). It was assigned construction number twenty-five. (Actually it was the forty-fourth locomotive produced by the firm, but a new serial numbering system had been started earlier that year, and so officially the *John Bull*'s maker's plate carried C/N 25.)[8]

After preliminary tests, the engine was disassembled and made ready for shipment. The boiler and cylinders could not be broken down further and were sent as a single unit, but all other parts were disassembled and packed into wooden boxes for shipment to Liverpool via a coastal vessel. Once in the major Atlantic port, the now-fragmented locomotive was placed aboard the *Allegheny,* which left Liverpool on July 14, 1831. The bill of lading is reproduced at right. The transportation charge was £19, equal to about $95.00 at the time. The bill for the locomotive itself came to £784 7s., or a little less than $4,000.

The *Allegheny* dropped its cargo at the Chestnut Street wharf in Philadelphia late in August. All of the pieces were then piled on a sloop that proceeded up the Delaware River to Bordentown. On reaching the waterfront of that small community on September 4, 1831, the boiler and the curious assemblage of boxes were unloaded. On shore ready to receive the cargo was Isaac Dripps, a young mechanic who had worked for the Stevens family since about 1829. Dripps, even at age twenty-one, was an experienced steamboat mechanic with a fine knowledge of practical steam engineering. Yet neither he nor any of his assistants had ever

SHIPPED, in good Order and Condition, by Francis B. Ogden in and upon the good Ship or Vessel called The Allegheny.........whereof Anthony Michaels......is Master, for this present voyage, now lying in the Port of LIVERPOOL, and bound for Philadelphia ......viz. One Locomotive Steam Engine as follows. One Engine Body, boiler &c shipped on deck.

Two pair large wheels and axles ..
Three Boxes .... Under deck
One Iron Box ....

being marked and numbered as per Margin; and are to be delivered, in the like good Order and Condition, at the aforesaid Port of Philadelphia (all and every the dangers and accidents of the Seas and Navigation, of whatsoever nature or kind, excepted) unto Edwin A. Stevens Esq. for the Camden and South Amboy R. Road & Trans Co—or to their Assigns; he or they paying freight for the said Goods Nineteen pounds Sterling .... with Primage and Average accustomed.
IN WITNESS whereof, the Master or Purser of the said Ship or Vessel hath affirmed to three Bills of Lading, all of this tenor and date; one of which being accomplished, the rest to stand void.—Dated in LIVERPOOL, this 14th Day of July—1831.

Contents unknown to
ANTHY. MICHAELS.

before seen a locomotive. One can imagine their sinking spirits on seeing the naked boiler and a pile of heavy wooden boxes rather than a fully assembled railway engine. They doggedly loaded up their dismembered charge on wagons and transferred it all to a short length of track near the town. No drawings or assembly instructions were enclosed in any of the boxes. Robert Stevens was absent on other business—he alone of anyone associated with the enterprise had at least seen a fully complete locomotive.

Over the next ten days Dripps managed to solve the puzzle and after some trial and error put the pieces together. Stevens was summoned to Bordentown for a preliminary trial. The boiler was filled with water and a fire was lit. When thirty pounds of steam were raised, Dripps and Stevens decided to open the throttle. To their delight, the engine moved forward along the test track. Yet all was not right, and some reassembly and adjustment were necessary before everything was in readiness. A tender was needed for fuel and water. A small four-wheel flatcar was fitted with a water tank improvised from a whiskey keg. A local shoemaker produced leather hoses to make flexible connections between the keg and intake pipes of the water pumps.

Stevens next decided to pay back some political debts by showing off his novelty. It would be the occasion for a grand party. On November 12, 1831, a Saturday, he invited members of the New Jersey legislature as well as a few local dignitaries, notably Napoleon's nephew, Prince Murat.[9] The prince's wife hurried aboard the cars, determined to be the first woman to travel on a steam-powered train. Stevens thought it important to impress the most influential people of the state with this new marvel of the age. It was a festive occasion, with a bountiful table to reassure the timid that

Figure 7. Isaac Dripps (1810–1892) assembled the *John Bull* after its arrival from England. He was one of the first American railway master mechanics. (*Inventive Age*, November 17, 1891.)

the age of steam would also encompass the more traditional pleasures of everyday life. Many trips were made back and forth on the test track, much to the delight of the assembled guests. The party continued late into the night at a local hotel. One of the enthusiastic participants, a local worthy named Obediah Herbert, wrote to his son on the following day, saying:

> With much satisfaction and inexpressible surprise I received your letter (dated at New Orleans the 24th of October) on Tuesday the 10th inst. two days less than one month from the day you started from New York, I did not expect a letter until the last of this month.
>
> I should have written you immediately on the receipt of your letter, but there was a celebration—or first trial of the Steam Carriage on the railroad near Bordentown on Sat. the 12th inst. I went to see the exhibition and write some of the particulars to you. They had a coach that held thirty passengers attached to the steam car and ran one and a quarter miles in two minutes and twenty two seconds. This they repeated a great many times, as there was great assemblage of people there and all wanted to ride. The legislature was invited and attended in a body, and a great many of the best people in New Jersey. Robert Stevens conducted the machinery himself. It was a fine performance and gave great satisfaction.

After the excitement of the public demonstration was over, the *John Bull* was stored in a wooden shed awaiting completion of the railway. There it stood for nearly eighteen months, for although portions of the line were completed, horses rather than locomotives were used for motive power.

A single locomotive could not service the line, and

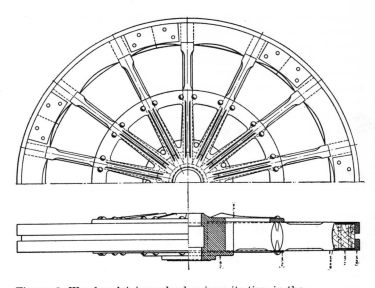

Figure 8. Wooden driving wheel, minus its tire, in the Smithsonian's railroad collection.

Stevens was busy building more engines. By the spring of 1833 enough had been assembled to assist in construction. Two purposes were served—yeoman work in moving materials and practical engine running experience for the inexperienced crews. (There were no experienced operating men to be hired at any price.) Stevens must have recognized the dangers of operating horse-drawn cars and steam-powered trains on a single-track railway. When the conversion came, it must be done at once. Men and machines must be ready for the transition.

During the training period, the *John Bull* broke its crank axle while backing around a curve. It was too light, 3¼ inches in diameter. A new axle, made one-half-inch heavier, was ordered. It is likely that during this repair session Stevens made the first of many modifications to the *John Bull*. He had publicly demonstrated a cowcatcher of his design in June 1833. The device was more than a barrier to push obstacles off the track; it was also meant to steer the locomotive into and out of curves by means of a pair of small leading or pilot wheels. A heavy wooden frame, carried at one end by leading wheels and at the other end by bearings mounted on the extended ends of the front driving wheels, worked to shift or guide the front drivers on curves (figs. 9 and 11). The pilot could be detached from the locomotive by unbolting the bearing caps. Handles were provided at the end of the frame near the driving-axle bearing so that two men could wheel it away from the engine once it was detached. All of this was necessary because the railroad employed turntables too short to handle the locomotive and its pilot. David Stevenson, a Scottish engineer, praised the device in *Civil Engineering in North America* (1838) by saying:

I experienced the good effects of it upon one occasion on the Camden and Amboy Railway. The train in which I travelled, while moving with considerable rapidity, came in contact with a large waggon loaded with firewood, which was literally shivered to atoms by the concussion. The fragments of the broken waggon, and the wood with which it was loaded, were distributed on each side of the railway, but the guard prevented any part of them from falling before the engine-wheels, and thus obviated what might in that case have proved a very serious accident.

Stevens himself described the scheme in the C&A's annual report of 1833 in the following words (the patent alluded to was, incidentally, never granted):

The ends of the axle extend beyond the carriage, and run in boxes, inserted in strong frame work which is projected in front of the carriage, and to which two smaller wheels are attached, adapted to the track. As the carriage is propelled forward, these guide wheels, which are of sufficient weight only to keep them on the rail, (so that the friction is comparatively nothing,) follow the track, and necessarily give the proper direction to the wheels of the carriage, and always preserve their parallelism with the rails. By this simple device the difficulty above alluded to is completely obviated, as the flanges of the carriage wheels can never come in contact with the edge of the rail. Both carriages of the American engines are of this construction. Repeated experiments have been made with them, and the success uniform and complete. With one of them, a train of ten cars, containing stone and iron equal in weight to three hundred and forty passengers, has been propelled at a very high speed along the portions of the line, in which not only the greatest curvature, but the highest grade exist, without the slightest

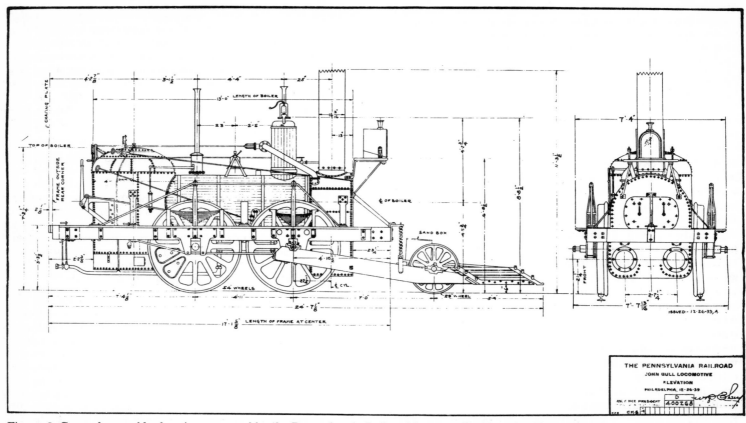

Figure 9. General assembly drawing prepared by the Pennsylvania Railroad in 1939. (Smithsonian Neg. 37,755.)

impediment or difficulty. In running them from Amboy to Bordentown, the flanges, in no instance, were found to come in contact with the rails, or to produce the least resistance, although the greatest curves in the line, in many instances at a speed exceeding thirty miles per hour. A patent will be obtained by Mr. Stevens, for the purpose of securing the benefits of this invention to himself and the Company.

It was necessary to remove the outside cranks and side rods to mount the cowcatcher-pilot. This naturally rendered the front driving wheels powerless and transformed the *John Bull* into a peculiar machine that seems to defy the Whyte locomotive classification system. Is a 2-2-2-0 to be believed? Yet the machine is surely not a 2-4-0 as it might appear, since the former front drivers are now only a set of carrying wheels.

Once the tinkering began it seemingly never ceased. Stevens and Dripps were overflowing with ideas to improve the handiwork of Robert Stephenson. Some of their ideas were sound, but others were simply awful. The bell, headlight, and whistle made good sense for the unfenced tracks and grade-level road crossing typical of our pioneer railroads. The ability both to see and warn trespassers was essential. The later addition of a cab to protect the engineer was humanitarian. The substitution of inside iron frames for the wooden original produced a more solid foundation and gave extra inches of free space where it was so very much needed, inside of the driving wheels. Moving the springs above the axles and reinforcing the outside wooden frame with an iron truss or hog brace made sense. The merits of the new lever-operated valve gear were less obvious but may have had some advantages over the original

shifting eccentric gear. The funnel-shaped smokestack with its internal spark-arresting apparatus was another perfectly rational modification needed to transform a British locomotive into something suitable for American use. However, what makes no sense was the removal of the throttle valve from its original position inside the boiler. Elevating the valve was wise—Stephenson's location was too low for the valve to draw most effectively from the driest steam available, and so the addition of the tall steamdome on the forward course of the boiler waist was admirable (figs. 1 and 10). However, the throttle valve was mounted *outside* the dome and the dry pipes arched out into mid-air before plunging through the roof of the smokebox to the valve boxes. The valve and the dry- (or steam-delivery) pipes were without benefit of insulation. In their breezy perch on top of the boiler they were rapidly cooled, thus lessening the power and efficiency of the engine. The heat loss during the winter, particularly when running fast, must have been substantial. It was about the worst imaginable drypipe arrangement from a thermodynamic standpoint.

An examination of the engine reveals other alterations or inconsistencies when compared with the scant documentation available on its mechanical history. The cylinder size, one of the most basic of all locomotive measurements, is a case in point. Contemporary records, such as Stevens's memo and the Stephenson specifications, give the size as a 9-inch bore and a 20-inch stroke. This statistic was never questioned and appeared in early literature and labels printed by the Pennsylvania Railroad and the United States National Museum. However, the 1853 annual report of the Camden and Amboy gives the cylinder size as 11½ by 20 inches. In recent years one cylinder head was removed, re-

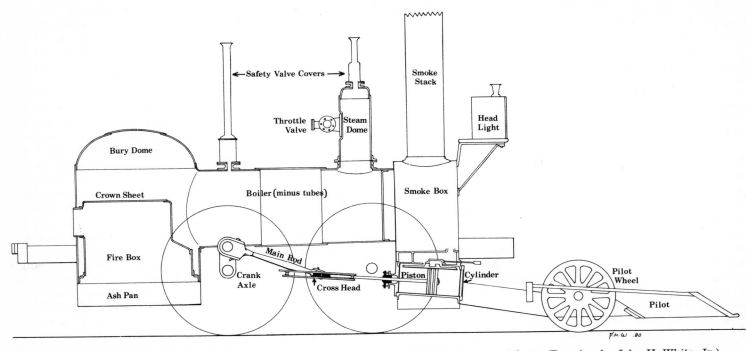

Figure 10. Longitudinal cross section shows the principal parts of the *John Bull* in its present form. (Drawing by John H. White, Jr.)

vealing a true measurement of 11 by 20 inches. Just to add to the confusion, an Austrian engineer named Von Gerstner, who visited the C&A in about 1839, gave the cylinder size as 11 by 16 inches in a book published on American railroads just a few years after his visit.[10] It is possible that some of this confusing data could be explained by the speculation that the *John Bull* was delivered with 9-x-20-inch cylinders and that they were replaced with a larger pair sometime before 1853. The smokebox has been deepened by 3 inches, which helps to support this theory.

The boiler-tube data is similarly confused. The original specifications call for 82 tubes with an outside diameter of 1⅝ inches. Watkins claimed in his booklet of 1891 that the boiler contained only 62 tubes with 2-inch diameters; he does not specify whether the measurement was inside or outside calibration. (He is, incidentally, 1 foot in error on the boiler diameter, listing it as 3 feet 6 inches rather than 2 feet 6 inches, which makes one rather skeptical of his mechanical report.) In 1962 the present writer removed the smokebox to discover 74 iron tubes measuring 1⅝ inches inside diameter.

The valve gear mentioned earlier in this discussion is one of the best-hidden mechanical features of the *John Bull,* being buried between the double frames, very near the engine's center line. The original mechanism was a stock, shifting eccentric gear devised by Stephenson. A foot treadle on the floor of the deckplate was connected by a series of rods and levers to the two loose eccentrics on the rear driving axle. The engine could be placed in forward or reverse motion by moving the eccentric through the medium of the foot treadle.[11] This arrangement was later replaced by the present valve gear, which basically dispensed with the loose eccentrics and foot treadle for a reach-rod system. Two fixed eccentrics are connected to a rocker shaft mounted on the lower front of the smokebox by two flat rods. These rods are bent to reach over or under the axles—they pass through the smokebox between the cylinders. The ends of these rods are made as open U-hooks that can engage pins on the rocker levers. Rods running over the top of the boiler to small bell cranks on the top front of the smokebox raise or lower the hooks to engage or disengage the lever pins. Thus when the upper pin is engaged the engine moves forward and when the lower pin is engaged the machine is put in reverse. There is also a neutral position when neither pin is engaged. There are three notches in the firebox end of the reach rod (fig. 11). These notches inform the engineer of the valve's position and also hold the mechanism in place. Each valve must be moved individually, making it possible to have one valve set forward and the other in reverse.

Because it is necessary to adjust the position of the rockers to engage the gear, two shifting levers are connected to the rocker shaft by rods that extend, on an angle from the shaft fastened to the rear of the firebox, to the front of the locomotive. These rods are rather hard to see because they are placed behind the driving wheels (figs. 9 and 11). The levers are worked independently in concert with the lifting rods. A skilled engineer could manually operate the valves through these levers by disengaging the eccentric rods and setting the lifting rods in the middle or neutral position. Manual operation was useful when the engine was being positioned on a turntable or under a water tank. The valve gear was simple but far from ideal. It was difficult to manage because the engineer could not see what

E.E.7643

he was doing and had to manipulate the hooks and levers by "feel." With engines fitted with V-hook or link-motion valve gears, it was mechanically impossible to reverse the valve when the engine was running fast, a course of action occasionally necessary for emergency stops.[12] There was also a constant danger to the operating crew, for the shifting levers could not be disengaged but were constantly in motion when the engine was running. They rocked back and forth at a ferocious pace in a lethal scissors action endangering all who came near them. Yet they stood exposed and unguarded in the immediate work area of both the fireman and engineer.

An inspection of the *John Bull* would convince anyone with a mechanical sense that many changes were made during its long years of service. Coverplates, studs, and an occasional small fitting or broken-off bracket are mute evidence of a continuing metamorphosis. The documentary scraps available also testify to the many changes previously outlined, but the records are far from complete and in a few particulars they are even contradictory. Sadly, we cannot with much assurance state just when most alterations were made. Isaac Dripps prepared a brief memorandum in 1885 that lists the changes, but he does not tell us when they happened, except in the case of the crank axle.[13] From circumstantial evidence we can be rather certain that the pilot was added at the same time, about 1833. It is probable that the bell, whistle, and maybe even the headlight were added by 1840. The cab most likely did not appear until about

Figure 12. The reversing levers can be seen on the left side of this photograph. They are always in motion when the engine is running and present a hazard to the operating crew. (Courtesy of the Pennsylvania Railroad.)

Figure 11. This broadside photograph, believed to have been taken in 1927, clearly shows some of the mechanical features of the *John Bull*. (Courtesy of the Pennsylvania Railroad.)

1850. The eight-wheel tender was probably added at roughly the same time. There was one group of components that Dripps was more careful to date, perhaps because they were such a troublesome problem to solve. The original wooden wheels were reinforced with iron crank rings and plates. Stevens alluded to Jones's iron wheels in his memo of 1830, but apparently Stephenson prevailed and supplied his standard wooden pattern.[14] The locust wheels were not strong enough and worked loose after only one year's service. One of these wheels, minus its flanged tire, is in the Smithsonian's collection (fig. 8). Dripps next tried metal wheels with round spokes riveted to the rims, but they too worked loose after a brief period. In about 1835 cast-iron wheel centers were adopted. Today the engine has cast-iron wheels with H-pattern spokes that may date from this period. Curiously, the left front wheel varies slightly in appearance from its mates. The tires are wrought iron and are shrunk onto the centers.

An occasional visitor will question the whereabouts of the brake rigging for the *John Bull*. The answer is simple: none exists and none was ever applied. The *John Bull* and its nineteenth-century counterparts were devoid of brakes. The engine was meant to propel and not stop the train. Before the air brake, the brakes and brakemen were on the cars. The engineer's only association with this mechanism was his whistle, which he would blow as a signal that it was necessary to slow down or stop.

Locomotive superintendents were passionately opposed to brakes for their engines. This was the responsibility of the master car builder. Brake shoes would cut away and ruin the profile of driving-wheel tires. They would push the axles out of alignment and ruin the axle and connecting-rod bearings. Brake rigging was a needless appendage to the locomotive, which already was overburdened with auxiliary apparatus. It was not until the 1870s that this prejudice was overcome and brakes were applied to locomotives as well as cars, but of course by that time the *John Bull* was in retirement.

Tender brakes were another matter. A tender was, after all, more analogous to a car, and a car might properly be fitted with brakes. It was convenient to be able to stop the engine on those occasions when it moved about without a train of cars. It was also helpful to be able to hold the engine at stations, water tanks, or fueling places. And in an emergency the tender brake was used by the fireman to avoid the embarrassment of a collision. But tender brakes were usually minimal and no doubt reflected the contempt locomotive men had for stopping rather than going. The brakes on the *John Bull* tender are modest indeed. A curved wooden block or shoe is manually pressed against each wheel tread. Each pair of wheels is braked independently. The front set is worked by a long lever inside of the tender body, while the rear pair is activated by a foot pedal pushed by the brakeman stationed in the gig seat on top of the tender roof.

Service and Exhibition History

The *John Bull* saw very limited service until the fall of 1833, when the regular operation of steam trains began over completed portions of the line. By the late 1840s new locomotives began to relegate the *John Bull* to less prestigious duties. In 1849 the road's premier engine was being used in Bordentown, New Jersey, as a pump for hydrostatic tests of new boilers. An old C&A engineer who began

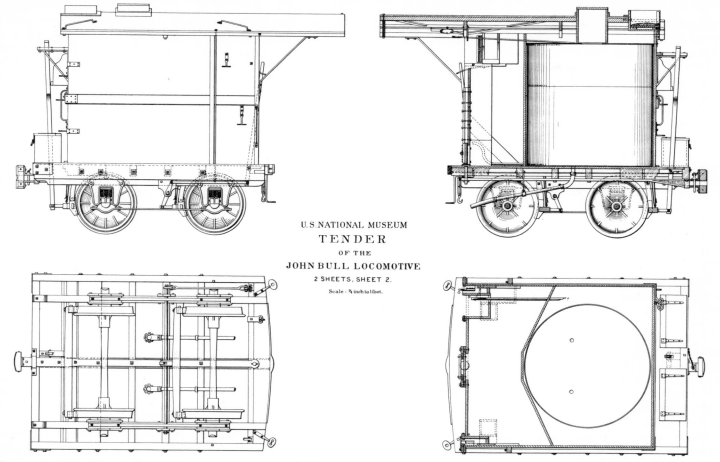

U.S. NATIONAL MUSEUM

TENDER

OF THE

JOHN BULL LOCOMOTIVE

2 SHEETS, SHEET 2.

Scale : ¾ inch to 1 foot.

Figure 13. The tender provided fuel and water as well as the only brakes associated with the engine. (Drawing by Charles H. Ourand.)

service around 1855 recalled operating the *John Bull* as a switcher in the Bordentown area.[15] He stated that the engine was also used to pull gravel or work trains and was last used to power a saw used for cutting firewood. An early photograph of the *John Bull* in its modernized form, with two cars, suggests that the engine was used in local train service, a very normal assignment for obsolete equipment (fig. 14). By 1858, even though it was still on the active roster, the engine had achieved the status of an antique. It was exhibited at the New Jersey State Agricultural Fair in Trenton. A diploma was given to the Camden and Amboy's relic at a time when the railroad was hardly beyond its infancy and only a few locomotives were seen beyond the Mississippi River. In fact a number of the *John Bull's* sisters had already been retired or sold off for secondary service elsewhere. Yet the Stevens family was still in command, and though Robert L. Stevens was deceased, other members of the clan retained a sentimental regard for the veteran. It was with some wonderment that the *American Railway Review* for April 25, 1861, announced that, "considering the value of old iron," the Camden and Amboy had "layed up in ordinary the old 'John Bull' . . . " Five years later the engine was retired from regular service and set aside permanently. It is only by chance that it escaped the junkman's hammer after the Pennsylvania Railroad leased the property in 1871. The Standard Railroad of the World was hardly a hotbed of sentimentalists. It was in fact governed by eminently practical technicians who quickly decimated the C&A's stock of aging locomotives and cars. Angus Sinclair lamented the rampant utilitarianism among railway managers and claimed some "were the kind of men who would readily melt the Liberty Bell for the metal it contains."[16]

Yet some anonymous protector saved the *John Bull,* and it remained hidden away at Bordentown until the time of the United States Centennial. The national anniversary celebration prompted the hard-nosed managers of the Pennsylvania to think about their beginnings, and it was decided to refurbish the old *John Bull* and two antique coaches. However, the engine appeared a trifle too modern, and except for its size, most visitors to the fair would hardly have noticed a remarkable difference between a forty-five-year-old relic and the engines operating on the main line. The shops were put to work "restoring" the No. 1. Off came the cab and the bonnet stack. A straight stack with a serrated crown, inspired presumably by the *Locomotion,* was put on. (This makeshift stovepipe was like nothing ever carried by the locomotive during its service career, but because it has been in place for over a century, it is now a permanent feature of the engine's profile.) The eight-wheel tender was too grand and modern and was cut down to a four-wheel vehicle. It is not based on any known prototype. A spoked pair of leading wheels replaced the solid-plate wheels. Because the engine, with its pair of ancient coaches, was taken to the fairgrounds under its own steam, a modern steam gauge was added for safety.[17] The *John Bull* thus survives today not as it appeared during its service life (1831–66) but as the mechanics of Bordentown remodeled it in 1876. Two views of the engine at the Centennial are known to survive (figs. 15 and 16). In the following year the *Railroad Gazette* printed an engraving and a brief history of the engine that have confused historians for decades. The line cut shows the engine with its cab and double-truck tender. One would naturally assume that this was the

Figure 14. The *John Bull* and two early cars in a photograph made after the end of its service life. (Chaney Neg. 14,489.)

Figure 15. The Pennsylvania Railroad featured the *John Bull*, suitably antiqued, at the 1876 Centennial Exhibition in Philadelphia. (Smithsonian Neg. 80-20784.)

way it appeared in 1877; however, the engraver was working from an old photograph and not from life (fig. 17).[18] Here is another example of the pitfalls awaiting the uncritical researcher.

Misguided as the 1876 remodeling might now appear, this action helped establish the *John Bull* as a national relic. At the same time it was returned to operating condition and moved under its own power to Philadelphia. In tow were two period coaches. The ancient train was shown on a track on the Centennial grounds. The railroad industry, still growing, was beginning to exploit its past for public-relations purposes. Nearby at the Maryland Pavilion, the Baltimore and Ohio placed one of its pioneer *Grasshopper*-type locomotives on display. But the other Centennial railway exhibits emphasized the present and future, in keeping with the nation's self-image as Young America.

After the Centennial the *John Bull* was returned to storage, presumably at Bordentown. The facility was closed by the Pennsylvania and stood idle until 1881, when it was leased to a private firm. At this time the *John Bull* was moved to the Meadows shops in Kearny, New Jersey. In September of the following year the directors of the Pennsylvania took time to ponder the future of the relic. They concluded that they were in the transportation and not the museum business and quite sensibly voted to donate the locomotive to the Smithsonian Institution. The museum accession file records this action but does not document just how vigorously the offer was pressed or just why it was declined. The apparent reason was that the institution simply was not ready to accept engineering specimens and was determined to concentrate only on natural-history subjects, together with a few miscellaneous relics inherited from

1314 — THE FIRST LOCOMOTIVE AND TRAIN

Figure 16. The *John Bull* train on exhibit at the U.S. Centennial grounds in 1876. (Smithsonian Neg. 74-3812-27.)

Figure 17. This photograph shows the *John Bull* at about the time of its retirement in 1866. Ten years later the bonnet stack and the cab were removed and the eight-wheel tender was cut down to a four wheeler in an effort to make the machine look less modern. (Chaney Neg. 8810.)

other government agencies, such as the Patent Office.

Meanwhile, a major show, the National Railway Appliance Exposition, was being organized in Chicago. It was scheduled to open in May 1883, and its backers were seeking modern and early exhibits. They succeeded admirably and mounted an even larger railway display than that assembled for the Centennial. The supply-trade industry filled the exhibit galleries with the latest in track tools, signals, locomotives, and cars. One part of the floor was named the Old Curiosity Shop and was set aside for rare, aged mementos of the railway age. The North Eastern Railway sent the *Locomotion* (1825) all the way from England. The Chicago and North Western pulled its *Pioneer* out of the boneyard for display at the lakefront fairground. And of course the Pennsy sent its representative to the Old Curiosity Shop.

After the Chicago exhibit closed, the railroad again wondered what to do with the *John Bull*. It faced another minor problem as well: what to do with a young civil engineer named J. Elfreth Watkins (1852–1903) who had lost a leg in an accident on one of its New Jersey lines. Watkins was no longer fit for fieldwork but he had a passion for engineering history. This interest was not too useful for the engineering department of the powerful Pennsy but it might be well employed by the Smithsonian, which was now expressing a mild interest in expanding its collections to include technology. In 1884 Watkins was detailed by the railroad to work at the Smithsonian's Arts and Industries Building, opened in 1880 to house materials displayed at the Centennial. Watkins was hardly aboard when talks began anew about transferring the *John Bull*. Because no exhibit space was immediately available, the locomotive was stored temporarily in a shed on the Armory grounds located across the street from the museum. At last it had reached a safe haven and was forever removed from the unpredictable humor of a presiding master mechanic who might, on a whim, send the useless junker to the scrapyard. As the Smithsonian's first engineering specimen the *John Bull* became something of a celebrity in the museum world. On December 22 it was placed on exhibit in the East Hall of the Arts and Industries Building and was proclaimed by one enthusiastic reporter as the ancestor of all American locomotives.[19] Here it stayed, except for a few outside loans, until 1964, when it was removed to the National Museum of American History.

The *John Bull* did leave the security of the museum on a few occasions. The most notable came in 1893, when it was taken out to participate in the Columbian Exposition. The Pennsylvania Railroad, together with many other large American business firms, agreed to mount major displays at the Chicago fair. Because the exposition was to be a show of the new and the old, the *John Bull* was seen as the ideal representative for the latter category. Sometime in February the locomotive was taken to the railroad's Jersey City shops, where it was reconditioned under the supervision of the chief mechanical officer, Theodore N. Ely. The railroad planned a publicity stunt of no mean proportions. It would run the old engine and two veteran coaches from Jersey City to Chicago. The thousand-mile trip was sure to excite public interest. Was the well-worn machine ready for the longest trip of its career, after not turning a wheel for nearly twenty years? Ely and his men made what repairs seemed necessary and took the *John Bull* out on the old line to Perth Amboy. She steamed over the fifty-mile route in

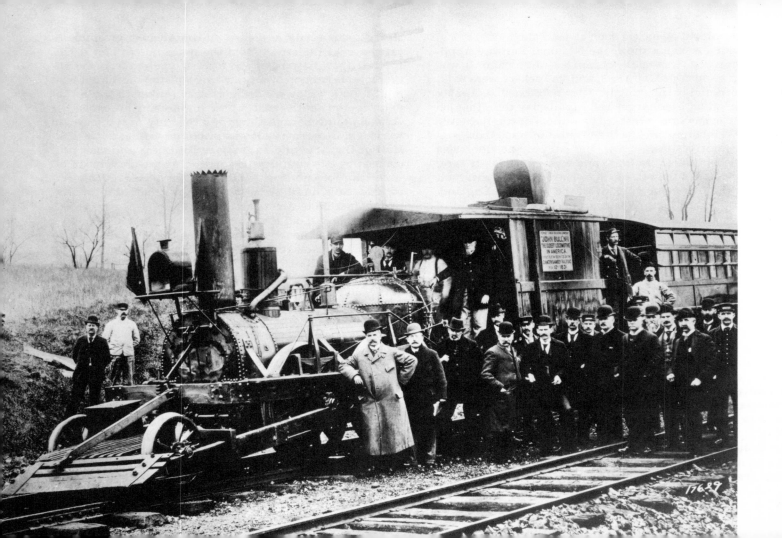

Figure 19. The schedule for the *John Bull*'s longest journey, made nearly thirty years after its retirement from active service.

SCHEDULE
OF THE
JOHN BULL SPECIAL TRAIN
New York to Chicago,
APRIL 17th to 22d, 1893.

EAST OF PITTSBURG.

MONDAY, APRIL 17th.

Lv. New York	10.00 A. M.
Jersey City	10.16 "
Newark	10.40 "
Elizabeth	11.09 "
Rahway	11.40 "
New Brunswick	12.25 P. M.
Trenton	2.07 "
Bristol	2.45 "
Tacony	3.35 "
Ar. Philadelphia, Broad St. Station	4.40 "
Lv. " "	6.46 "
Downingtown	8.55 "
Coatesville	9.20 "
Lancaster	11.30 "

TUESDAY, APRIL 18th.

Lv. Middletown	1.40 A. M.
Steelton	2.05 "
Ar. Harrisburg	2.15 "
Lv. "	7.00 "
Marysville	7.28 "
Duncannon	7.58 "
Newport	8.59 "
Mifflin	10.45
Lewistown Junction	11.31 A. M.
McVeytown	12.17 P. M.
Huntingdon	2.05 "
Tyrone	3.45 "
Bellwood	4.15 "
Ar. Altoona	4.45 "
Lv. "	6.00 "
Johnstown	10.00 "

WEDNESDAY, APRIL 20th.

Lv. Blairsville Int.	12.10 A. M.
Derry	12.50 "
Latrobe	1.35 "
Greensburg	2.25 "
Jeannette	3.00 "
Irwin	3.30 "
Braddock	4.30 "
Wilkinsburg	4.50 "
Ar. Pittsburg	5.25 "

SCHEDULE
OF THE
JOHN BULL SPECIAL TRAIN
New York to Chicago,
APRIL 17th to 22d, 1893.

WEST OF PITTSBURG.

WEDNESDAY, APRIL 20th.

Lv. Pittsburg, Central time	8.00 A. M.
Rochester, Pa	10.05 "
New Brighton, Pa	10.20 "
Beaver Falls, Pa	10.30 "
Leetonia, Ohio	1.20 P. M.
Salem, Ohio	1.50 "
Alliance, Ohio	3.15 "
Canton, Ohio	4.45 "
Massillon, Ohio	5.25 "
Ar. Orrville, Ohio	6.35 "

THURSDAY, APRIL 20th.

Lv. Orrville, Ohio	8.00 A. M.
Wooster, Ohio	9.00 "
Mansfield, Ohio	12.10 P. M.
Lv. Crestline, Ohio	1.30 "
Bucyrus, Ohio	3.00 "
Upper Sandusky, Ohio	4.15 "
Forest, Ohio	5.10 "
Ada, Ohio	6.20 "
Ar. Lima, Ohio	7.30 "

FRIDAY, APRIL 21st.

Lv. Lima, Ohio	8.00 A. M.
Delphos, Ohio	9.05 "
Van Wert, Ohio	10.10 "
Fort Wayne, Ind	1.05 P. M.
Columbia City, Ind	2.35 "
Warsaw, Ind	4.10 "
Ar. Plymouth, Ind	6.35 "

SATURDAY, APRIL 22d.

Lv. Plymouth, Ind	8.00 A. M.
Valparaiso, Ind	11.05 "
Ar. Chicago, Ill	3.00 P. M.

Figure 18. On the road bound for the Columbian Exposition in April 1893. The *John Bull* left its haven at the Smithsonian for eight months.

Figure 20. Once at the 1893 exposition, the engine and its two ancient coaches offered rides to visitors. (Courtesy of F.W. Blauvelt.)

just two hours and fifteen minutes.

Ely was confident that all was now in readiness and proudly exhibited his antique train on Hudson Street in Jersey City. On Monday morning, April 17, 1893, the train left for the West. President Cleveland was invited to ride, as were the governors of the states to be traversed by the train. We have no record if any of these dignitaries accepted Ely's offer, but the press and lesser folk were delighted to receive tickets. A modern locomotive and dining and sleeping car followed the old train to provide for the crew and passengers. A. S. Herbert, an engineer since the early 1850s, operated the engine. J. W. Sanford and G. W. Zengel served as firemen. Once beyond Philadelphia, local-division engine men familiar with the trackage rode on the footplate acting as pilots. The schedule was intentionally leisurely because of the equipment's age and the desire to give the local populace an opportunity to view the train en route. Frequent stops were made, and in those towns not so favored, the speed was reduced to three or four miles an hour. (A schedule of the train appears in fig. 19.) The engine ran along easily at twenty-eight to thirty miles an hour. No mechanical problems were encountered.

The quaint, living exhibit was successful in attracting the curious. Enthusiasm ran high at some locations. At Johnstown, Pennsylvania, for example, a large crowd reinforced by a brass band was waiting outside the depot at midnight when the *John Bull* steamed into view. After reaching Chicago on April 22, the train moved out to the lakefront grounds of the exhibition. It operated on an outdoor track adjacent to Pennsylvania's display building (fig. 20). Rides were given to thousands of visitors. The return trip began on December 6. A slightly different route was

Figure 21. The Baltimore and Ohio Railroad produced a pageant in 1927 to honor the line's 100th anniversary, which included the *John Bull* under steam. (Chaney Neg. 13,758.)

Figure 22. On November 12, 1931, the *John Bull*'s centenary was celebrated in the wonderful clutter of the Arts and Industries Building's East Hall, home to the engine since 1885. Frank Taylor stands on the floor; Jack Dorsey is on the runningboard. Both men were employees of the Smithsonian.

followed, with the train proceeding on the main line to Harrisburg, where it branched off on the Northern Central Railroad (another PRR subsidiary) and proceeded to Baltimore, where it again moved over the main line to Washington. It arrived on December 13, 1893.

After dropping the fire and draining the boiler, the *John Bull*'s crew returned the locomotive to the East Hall. To save floorspace, the tender was exhibited outside the Arts and Industries Building. The weather took its toll, and the tender was removed from public view and placed in the Ninth Street Annex; no one knows if it was under roof. In April 1909 it was moved again, this time to a temporary shed near the new National Museum of Natural History Building. An examination revealed serious deterioration of the wooden and metal parts. It was decided to dismantle the vehicle and save the sound pieces. Before this was done in October 1910, photographs and measured drawings were made. The roof and end of the body were so rotted that most or all of these segments were discarded. The circular iron water tank was badly rusted; a large hole near the bottom of its eaten-away plating was evident on one side. The side panels and larger pieces of ironwork, such as the draw bar, were in reasonably good condition. The nuts, bolts, and other pieces were packed in tool chests or crates. All salvaged materials were stored in the west end of the Smithsonian Institution Building. There they would remain for twenty years, dusty and forgotten. More years passed with the *John Bull* standing alone in the East Hall as the Smithsonian's sole railroad relic of any consequence, save for a few small artifacts and some models. The monotony was broken at last in 1927, when the engine was once again removed by the Pennsylvania Railroad. In 1927 the

Baltimore and Ohio would observe the centenary of its charter. Times were good, and the railroad decided to stage a lavish birthday party that would include a festive outdoor pageant enlivened by a parade of modern and historic locomotives and cars. The directors of the B&O invited the railroad industry to join them at Halethorp, Maryland (near Baltimore) for the Fair of the Iron Horse. The Pennsylvania agreed to exhibit the *John Bull* and one of the cars used on the 1893 train.[20] A replica tender was produced at the Altoona shops. The locomotive, on loan from the Smithsonian, was refurbished at the same facility before being sent to Baltimore. The engine operated under steam at the Fair of the Iron Horse, September 24 to October 15, 1927—the last time it did so until the test in October 1980 (*see* Appendix A).

In 1930 the officials of the Smithsonian found the pieces from the 1876 tender and asked the Altoona shops if they would build a second reproduction using these fittings. The reproduction was made, and it is this second replica that is in the present collection. During the next year the museum decided to celebrate the *John Bull*'s centenary. But these were the depression years, and in 1931 no funds were available for an elaborate celebration. The staff was determined not to let the event pass without notice, and with the modest means available, Frank A. Taylor put together a program. The replica tender was moved behind the locomotive. The 1836 coach borrowed from the PRR was put in place behind the tender (fig. 22). No money was available to steam the engine or remove it from the museum, so Taylor decided to operate it, in place, with compressed air. Even this modest proposal was considered too costly. Taylor would not give up. He found an existing air supply in the

Natural History Building and persuaded the maintenance crew to run a small copper tube through a heating tunnel across the Mall and into the East Hall. The tube was too small to deliver much in the way of volume, but given enough time, a sufficient head of air could be built up to turn the wheels. The rear wheels were jacked up to clear the rails. Taylor chose November 12, the date of the public demonstration in 1831, as the engine's official birthday. With coach, tender, and air line in place, he invited a radio announcer, Stanley Bell of CBS, to broadcast the *John Bull*'s story. With the sounds of the bell, whistle, and exhaust in the background, Bell dramatically narrated to the nation at large the history of the iron horse.

Two years later the Pennsylvania borrowed the *John Bull* for an exhibit at the Century of Progress in Chicago. In 1939 the engine was taken to the New York World's Fair. In neither exhibit was it operated either by steam or compressed air. For reasons not reflected in the accession papers, either the museum or the railroad decided that further operation of the *John Bull* was not desirable. Accordingly, a full-sized steamable replica was produced at the Altoona shops in 1939–40. This duplicate was operated at the 1940 New York World's Fair and the 1948 and 1949 Railroad Fair in Chicago. For some years afterwards it was stored in Northumberland, Pennsylvania. In recent years it was placed on exhibit at the Pennsylvania State Railroad Museum in Strasburg.

The original *John Bull* was to leave the East Hall once again late in 1939. It was taken to Wilmington, Delaware, for a parade. By this time the Smithsonian was seeing its first engineering specimen as perhaps too fragile and valuable for life on the road, and it remained well protected inside the East Hall until 1964, when it was moved to the then-new National Museum of History and Technology (today the National Museum of American History). Here it was incorporated within a new exhibit called *The Growth of the United States* that presented a capsule history of America through the more notable pieces in the collection. The labels for the exhibit moved the storyline forward without overwhelming the visitor with too much verbiage. The label for the *John Bull* explained in very general terms the rise of the railroad as representative of large corporations financed by multiple shareholders. Rather little was said about the locomotive itself. Some visitors were more puzzled than enlightened, and a number called my office in the museum's Division of Transportation seeking more specific information. One man called saying he had asked a guard to identify "that big black thing." The guard thought it was a steam engine or an old train. I answered that it was indeed a locomotive. Another visitor called insisting that some miscreant had slipped into the hall and switched all the labels around since none of them identified the objects they were standing by. A supplementary label was added to answer these complaints. When *The Growth of the United States* was closed to make way for another exhibit, the *John Bull* found new quarters in the main east hallway on the first floor near the pendulum.

Early in 1980 consideration was given to an appropriate commemoration of the *John Bull*'s impending 150th anniversary. We settled on September 15, the date of the first operation in North America, as the most meaningful date for an observance. But what to do? A publication and special exhibit were definitely in order. But what about operation? Preservation of an original is the first priority of all

REPLICA OF "JOHN BULL"
LOCOMOTIVE AND TENDER
BUILT AT ALTOONA WORKS.

Figure 23. In 1940 the Pennsylvania Railroad built a full-sized operating replica of the *John Bull* for exhibit purposes at public events such as world's fairs. (Courtesy of the Pennsylvania Railroad.)

responsible museums. For this reason, operation of such a valuable artifact is permissible only on a very limited basis and only if no existing parts are damaged or lost in the process. That much was understood by all involved in the project. No one had an accurate idea of the machine's physical condition. Numerous visual examinations over recent years confirmed that the engine was complete and sound, at least superficially. But were the working parts really in good order? We jacked the rear wheels off the track and cautiously turned them manually. The mechanism seemed free and well aligned. Next we decided to try compressed air. One morning in January 1980, before the museum opened to the public, a hose was attached to a temporary connection through the steamdome. The safety valves began to rattle and lift at forty-two pounds. The throttle was opened, and with a series of barks and snorts, sounding as though a weary dragon had been aroused, the ancient machine came to life. With the first exhaust puffs came a great cloud of dust and debris from inside the boiler and smokebox. The accumulation of fifty years was visually apparent. After a few more tests the running gear lumbered up and the old machine was ticking away like a well-oiled hall clock.

The running gear seemed serviceable but a larger question remained: what about the boiler? It is always the most troublesome part of a locomotive. Could we safely expect to put it under steam? We decided to ask the most prestigious firm in this specialized area, and the Hartford Steam Boiler Inspection and Insurance Company very kindly agreed to assist us. The tests occupied eight men for three days.[21] Magnaflux was used to find surface and subsurface cracks in the boiler-shell and running-gear parts. A large electro-magnet was held by hand against the surface of the metal to be tested. Fine iron particles were dusted over the test area. (Filings will stand up in a row on or above any cracks.) Ultrasonic testing was used to locate imperfections in metal parts by reflected ultra-high-frequency sound waves. This method was also used to measure the thickness of metal plates. Both results were displayed on separate meters or screens. Radiographics was the final method of testing employed. It is akin to the X-ray negatives used by dentists, but in this case the films were as large as fourteen by seventeen inches. These tests were performed between 6:30 P.M. and 4:00 A.M., outside regular hours, to avoid exposing visitors and museum staff to X-rays.

The following defects were uncovered. The top corner of the right main rod's front end was broken off, inside an area normally covered by the front-rod strap. This void would not prevent operation of the engine, but it was decided to fill it in by welding. One tube had a small crack in the rolled welt at the front tube sheet. Several cracks were found in the rear tube sheet just below the bottom row of tubes. The belly or bottom sheet of the rear-boiler shell course was found to be rather thin, in some places as little as .170 of an inch. Elsewhere the shell measured about one-quarter of an inch or between .245 and .290 inches. The X-ray film showed another potential problem on the right-hand side, where the rear-boiler course joins the firebox. There, several cracks between the rivets were evident. These defects came as no surprise; we were only grateful that nothing more serious was uncovered during the examination. None of the defects noted would prevent limited operations at reduced boiler pressure. Originally the *John Bull* steamed at 70 psi, and we were contemplating a pressure of only 50 psi. This reduction would have a very measured effect on performance and efficiency, but it would easily permit slow-speed operation of a single-car train on a nearly level track.

Following this investigation, several hydrostatic tests were made. So that all joints and rivets could be observed, it was necessary to remove the wooden jacket placed around the exterior of the boiler waist and the steamdome for insulation. This was carefully removed and boxed for preservation. It was so dry and charred that we were reluctant to reinstall it for operation. Under normal use, wooden lagging was expected to last no more than four years. We assume the present pine lagging dates from the 1876 or 1893 remodeling. Removal of the lagging revealed several interesting facts. The most important was that the waist of the boiler might be the original construction. It conforms with the Stephenson drawing of 1831 and exhibits such antique features as the 4½-inch-wide weltplate that connects the halfplates of the boiler cylinder (fig. 6). A replacement boiler would surely have avoided this weak feature. Larger boilerplate available in later years would have permitted each ring to be made from a single sheet, which strengthened and simplified fabrication. The oval plate riveted on the central ring indicates that the original manhole was removed when the steamdome was added. This again indicates that the boiler waist dates back to 1831. It was also noted that the forward bottom half ring was replaced at some time in the engine's history. The rivet heads do not match the cone-shaped heads evident in all other parts of the boiler. We suspect that this plate was replaced in 1876, 1893, or 1927, when the engine was being repaired for exhibit service.

The hydro test, like the others, showed the boiler to be in surprisingly good condition. The tubes were dry and tight. There was some weeping around a few joints and rivets inside the firebox. The only serious leak—and it was relatively minor—was found at the rear of the firebox near the point at which the draw-bar angle irons are riveted on. One inspector informally told me the boiler was in as good condition as many he saw in low-pressure service every day in the field. We now felt it was safe to operate the engine at low pressure and of course at a slow speed.

Returning to the original Camden and Amboy line would have been ideal for a reenactment, but portions of the railroad are now abandoned. It occurred to me that a similar piece of trackage lay within a few miles of the museum. The Chessie System's Georgetown Branch, originally completed by the B&O in 1909, runs from Georgetown along the Chesapeake and Ohio Canal through Chevy Chase, Maryland, to a junction on the main line about one mile west of the Silver Spring station. The southern end of the line parallels the Potomac River and the canal that is now an elongated public park. It must look something like the portions of the C&A that ran along the Delaware and Raritan Canal. Even discounting this similarity, it offered a picturesque and convenient track. The Smithsonian has been pleased by the enthusiastic cooperation of the Chessie System and its great kindness in permitting us to use this section of track. The reenactment is scheduled for September 15, 1981, at 11:00 A.M. Several trips with the *John Bull* and the C&A coach No. 3 will be made at that time, which we hope will be a fitting memorial for this historic locomotive that has, against so many odds, survived to celebrate its 150th year.

Notes

1. A. D. Turnbull, *John Stevens: An American Record* (New York, 1928).

2. Stevens's steam wagon had a single cylinder and a vertical water-tube boiler. A gear drive engaged a rack placed in the center of the circular track. Horizontal guide wheels and not flanges held the wagon on the track. Two relics, the boiler tubes and safety valve, are preserved by the Smithsonian. No contemporary drawings for the original wagon are known to exist. All models and illustrations, together with two full-sized replicas, are based on the verbal description given by one of Stevens's grandsons nearly sixty-five years later. The grandson depended on his recollection of an inspection made when he was eleven years of age.

3. *The Best Friend of Charleston* was a light four-wheel machine with inside cylinders, a crank axle, and a bottle-shaped vertical boiler. It was one of the very few vertical boiler engines made for main-line service. The universal plan was for horizontal boilers. This was true on a worldwide basis for steam locomotives.

4. J. G. H. Warren's *A Century of Locomotive Building* remains the best source for data on early Stephenson locomotive design. This classic work was reprinted (ca. 1970) by Augustus Kelly. See also L. T. C. Rolt, *The Railway Revolution: George and Robert Stephenson* (New York, 1960).

5. The *Liverpool* was tested on the L&M in November 1830 and underwent one or more rebuildings before it was ready for service. Even then it found no haven on a British line but was shipped to America, where it was used on the Petersburg Railroad in Virginia.

6. Nickolas Woods alludes to Jones's wheels in his 1832 edition of *A Treatise on Railways* (p. 80), noting that the patentees were from London. A patent for metal spoked wheels was issued to Theodore Jones on October 11, 1826.

7. The New Jersey State Agricultural Society awarded the C&A Railroad a certificate for the engine *John Bull* in 1858.

8. The serial number assignments are given in Marshall's *A History of the Locomotive Engine . . . to 1831*. Michael Bailey, a modern student of Stephenson's locomotive-building activities, determined that the *John Bull* was actually No. 44.

9. Napoleon's brother, Joseph Bonaparte, once the king of Naples and the Two Sicilies, and Spain, fled to the United States after Waterloo. He purchased a large estate near Bordentown and lived in "distinguished exile" with his former court, which included Prince Murat. In 1830 Joseph returned to Europe, hoping in vain to claim the French throne.

10. Franz A. R. Von Gerstner, *Die Innern Communication der Vereinigten Staaten von Nord Amerika* (Vienna, 1842–43), 2:87.

11. Warren explains the loose eccentric valve on p. 286.

12. See John H. White, Jr., *American Locomotives, 1830–1880: An Engineering History* (Baltimore, 1968), pp. 187–202, for data on locomotive valve gears.

13. Dripps's memo of September 1885 is in the Smithsonian Institution Archives.

14. See note 6.

15. *Trenton Journal*, 13 Mar. 1917, recollections of Benjamin F. Jobes.

16. Angus Sinclair, *Development of the Locomotive Engine* (New York, 1907), p. 366.

17. *Railroad Gazette*, 11 Feb. 1876, p. 67; ibid., 28 Apr. 1876, p. 183.

18. Ibid., 9 Mar. 1877, p. 105.

19. *Railway Age*, 31 Dec. 1885, p. 819.

20. The second (ca. 1836) coach disappeared sometime between 1907 and 1927.

21. Data for the inspection is summarized from a memo dated 17 Mar. 1980, by W. L. Withuhn, now on file in the *John Bull* accession papers, Smithsonian Insitution.

II. Locomotives of the Camden and Amboy Railroad

If a convention of the curious and odd amongst early American locomotives were ever assembled, it could find no better gathering place than the Bordentown shops of the Camden and Amboy. The Bordentown enginehouse was already an established residence for some of the most outlandish engines ever to see regular service in North America. Most trunklines tested an occasional maverick at some time in their histories, but the C&A exhibited a positive penchant for the unorthodox in wholesale lots. The *John Bull* was transformed by Messrs. Stevens and Dripps into such a weird hybrid that even Robert Stephenson might not have recognized his own offspring.

The homemade sisters of the *John Bull* were alike in their peculiarity and stood apart from the more typical 4-2-0's and 4-4-0's of the period. The eight-wheel, geared freight engines favored by the C&A began with an engine aptly named the *Monster.* The high-wheel Cramptons adopted for passenger service in the late 1840s were like a creation of Dr. Frankenstein and were seemingly assembled from castaway parts from several sources. One can never be sure if the pieces came from a steamboat, a pumping engine, or a steam laundry. Just how to explain this affinity for the unusual is difficult, but it most likely can be ascribed to the independent and imaginative thinking of Robert L. Stevens, aided and abetted by Isaac Dripps. Both men had a lively interest in mechanics, and both saw themselves as more than ordinary railway master mechanics. They devoted considerable time and energy to steamboat design as well and seemed determined to transfer this knowledge to the railway field. They were not ready to copy the classic simplicity of the American-type locomotive so universally accepted by their colleagues. Instead, they embarked on an

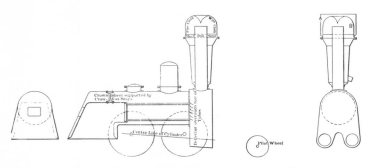

Figure 24. This outline drawing for one of the first C&A 2-2-2-0-type locomotives was published in the *Master Mechanics Report* for 1884 and is based on an original drawing supplied by Isaac Dripps.

independent course from the outset.

The first fifteen engines following the *John Bull* set something of a common standard. Weight and cylinder sizes varied somewhat, but all appear to have been of the 2-2-2-0 wheel arrangement established by the road's first engine. Five were produced by independent suppliers; the remainder were built in the C&A shops. To facilitate construction, Stevens ordered on March 16, 1832, ten pairs of 9-by-20-inch cylinders from Robert Stephenson, together with all other necessary parts except the boiler, chimney, frame, wheels, and firebars.[1] The first set of machined parts was shipped in early July 1832. The order was completed in February of the next year. Stevens felt the *John Bull* was a trifle too heavy and proposed to build on a lighter pattern. Eight engines were made on the scaled-down plan. Their weight has been estimated between five and eight tons; only Von Gerstner gives a precise figure of 13,692 pounds.[2] Both Von Gerstner and Knight and Latrobe agree that the driving wheels were 54 inches in diameter, which corresponds with the *John Bull*.[3] The first nine engines were fabricated at the old Stevens machine shop in Hoboken, which was set up mainly for steamboat repairs. The No. 16, the tenth and last company-produced machine of the set, was made at the railroad's new shop in Bordentown in 1836 or 1837. Precise delivery dates are uncertain, but we do know, from a newspaper account reproduced in the *American Railroad Journal,* that the third engine was ready for testing in June 1833.[4] This account mentions the leading wheels that enable the engine to traverse curves at 40 mph. Stevens boasted that his boiler produced nearly double the amount of steam generated by ordinary boilers—a claim not easily proved. The No. 3 burned a mix-

Figure 25. One of the C&A's original sixteen locomotives is shown in this lithograph of St. Mary's Church in Burlington, New Jersey, c. 1835. (Courtesy of the Old Print Shop.)

ture of wood and hard coal; plans were under way to develop a firebox to burn coal exclusively. The account closed by saying six or seven more engines would soon be ready.

While the family workshops were busy assembling engines, Stevens placed orders for five more with two outside suppliers. The first of these was Ezra K. Dod (1803–18?), a machinist from New York City, who was probably acquainted with the Stevens family as pioneer builders of steam engines.[5] His father, Daniel (1778–1823), had in fact played an active part in the design and construction of the machinery for the transatlantic steamer *Savannah* in 1819. Dod built locomotives Nos. 5 through 8 for the C&A in 1833 or 1834. An outline drawing for one of these machines was published in the 1884 *Master Mechanics Report* based on an original drawing then in the possession of Isaac Dripps (fig. 24). Dod may have supplied boilers for other company-built locomotives. The bonnet smokestack pictured in this drawing is the earliest representation known of this important style of spark arrester. Dod built no more locomotives for American lines. He emigrated to Cuba in about 1840, hoping the warmer climate would relieve his rheumatism. He continued as a mechanical engineer and became involved in the design and manufacture of sugar-mill machinery.

One more 2-2-2-0 was produced by another obscure New York machinist, Henry R. Dunham, proprietor of the Archimedes Works on North Moore Street.[6] Like Dod, Dunham's reputation was based on the manufacture of large marine engines. He was a supplier of such hardware to the Stevens family. Dunham expanded his operation in 1836 to include locomotive engines and during the next year completed the C&A's No. 15. Dunham is known to have built sixteen locomotives by 1838. No more appear to have been produced after that date, although Dunham remained active as a machinist until about 1856.

An old engineer named George Hollingsworth, once employed by the C&A, recalled that Stevens's diminutive fleet of inside-cylinder six-wheelers were good running engines.[7] But they were also difficult to reverse because of the peculiar valve gear. More particulars were supplied from an interview conducted with Stevens on November 25, 1837, by Knight and Latrobe:

> The number of locomotive engines owned by this company is 15, of which 12 are in constant use, averaging a running distance of 50 miles per day each. These engines weigh from 8 to 10 tons each, and have 4 wheels of an equal diameter of 4½ feet, with *pilot* wheels in front, that give direction to the foremost pair of the 4½ feet wheels, the latter being therefore not coupled with the remaining pair of 4½ feet or driving wheels. Each engine in the performance of the above named work of 50 miles per day, costs per annum about $4,000, including wages of enginemen at $50 per month, and of fireman at $35 per month, and cost of fuel, at the rate of three-fourths of a cord of wood for a run of 35 miles, including that consumed in getting up the steam, and waiting for steam boats. The day's work of each engineman and fireman is to run a passenger engine a circular trip of 70 miles between Amboy and Bordentown; and for any addition to such daily work they receive extra pay.

Von Gerstner's account, based on data gathered not long after the above report, adds a few other details. He states that steam pressure for all engines was 70 psi or about 20 pounds more than the British thought safe at that time. He incorrectly gives the *John Bull*'s cylinder size as 11 by 16 inches and claims all engines were made by Stevens except for the one of English manufacture. He gives the following cylinder sizes for the 2-2-2-0's but regrettably fails to note the road numbers involved:

Eight engines 9-x-20-inch cylinders
Three engines 9⅜-x-20-inch cylinders
Four engines 13-x-20-inch cylinders

Considering the obscurity and early date of these machines, we have a fair amount of data that is augmented considerably by an engraving and description of the No. 9, the *North America* (fig. 26).[8] The machine is pictured and described as it stood late in life when it had undoubtedly undergone some alterations. It was rebuilt in 1849 and may have been reboilered or enlarged at that time. Its weight was given as 12 tons and the cylinders measured 13 by 22 inches. The boiler was 39 inches in diameter by 96 inches long. It had eighty 2-inch tubes, each 72 inches long. Water grates suggest hard coal as the fuel. The exterior main frame and truck frame were wooden. The leading wheels were only 26 inches in diameter. The outside valve gear, long a favorite on the C&A when it was almost unknown on other American lines, is shown in the drawing. It might be noted that Nos. 12, 15, and 16 also had outside valve motions according to James White's recollection published in 1906.[9] The No. 9 was likely one of the last of the 2-2-2-0's in service when the aforementioned magazine article appeared in 1862. Many of her sisters had already been retired or sold several years earlier, and none are believed to have been on the roster after 1865.

While the last of the passenger engines were being bolted

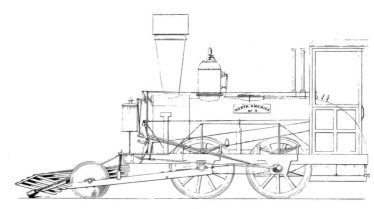

Figure 26. The *North America* is shown as it appeared not long before it was retired. Note the general similarity to the *John Bull* as it appeared c. 1866 (figure 17). (*American Railway Review*, May 8, 1862.)

Figure 27. A reconstruction of the original *Monster* built by the C&A between approximately 1835 and 1838. (*Locomotive Engineering*, February 1898.)

together, Stevens and Dripps were busy with drawings for a large freight locomotive. Nothing offered by the commercial shops satisfied them. They were determined to create something entirely original, and to that limited end they were successful. The No. 17 was envisioned as a coal-burning engine of great power and weight. Speed was not an important consideration. The resulting design called for a partially gear-driven 0-8-0 that weighed nearly three times as much as one of the passenger engines. The cumbersome mechanical arrangement, replete with such curious features as inclined cylinders and a pendulum or "horse's head" drive, so added to the machine's grossness that it was named the *Monster.*

Work on the *Monster* appears to have started as early as 1835.[10] Some parts were made in Hoboken, but final assembly was performed in Bordentown. The earliest contemporary account was that gathered by Knight and Latrobe in conversation with Stevens in November 1837. The men from Baltimore said the *Monster* was nearly completed. They gave the cylinders as 18 by 36 inches and estimated the weight at 18 tons. Von Gerstner gave the cylinders as 18 by 27 inches and gave the weight as 27 tons. While the precise dimensions are in question, any machine built within this size range would rank near the very top of the world's largest locomotives during the 1830s.

The *Monster*'s mechanical arrangement was even more astonishing than its size. Both the boiler and running gear were marvels of independent, if not necessarily practical, invention. The front pair of drivers were free to swivel to a limited degree, making the engine an articulated. The precise arrangement is uncertain—the assembly drawing reproduced here (fig. 28) does not show this detail—but we do have James White's description, made long years after the *Monster*'s retirement, in a 1906 newspaper article. White mentioned a heavy cast-iron saddle that served both as a support for the cylinders and a pivot point for the front drivers' independent frame. The connection between the saddle casting and the frame was made with centerplate and pin. Because the front drivers were articulated, it was not possible to connect the wheels to the rear set of drivers with the usual side-rod arrangement. Power was transmitted via broad face gears rather than side rods, mounted with ball-and-socket pins. The gear drive was not totally satisfactory because it worked under such a heavy strain that its teeth were occasionally stripped. When this unhappy occurrence was reported, old engineers on the line would tell their comrades that "John Holland or Dick Dayton had dropped his jewels."[11] The rear set of wheels was powered with conventional rods; however, the axle-box pedestals were fastened directly to the boiler!

The boiler was nearly equal to the running gear in its remoteness from orthodox design. It was built with a combustion chamber ahead of the firebox. A bridge or water partition separated the two chambers. A large pipe meant to improve circulation connected the crown sheet with the water leg of the partition (fig. 29). The engine steamed poorly as originally built. The basic problem was the difficulty in burning anthracite coal, a troublesome, slow-burning fuel that confounded the best efforts of most locomotive designers until around 1855. Stevens was interested in developing a plan to use anthracite because of the coal lands in Schuylkill County, Pennsylvania, purchased by the C&A Railroad in June 1835.[12] Mention was made earlier of attempts to use a mixture of wood and coal, but the *Monster*

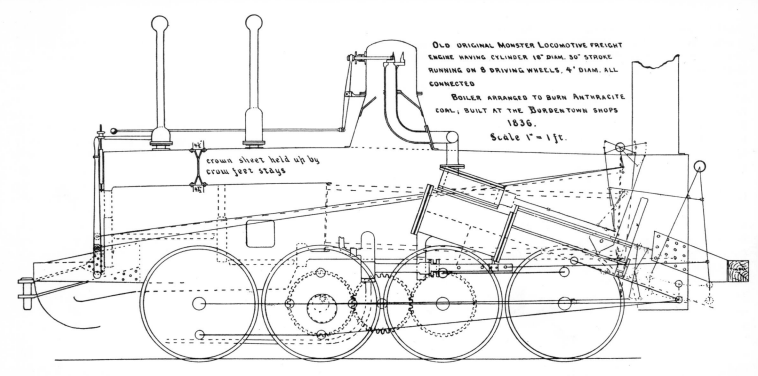

OLD ORIGINAL MONSTER LOCOMOTIVE FREIGHT
ENGINE HAVING CYLINDER 18" DIAM. 30" STROKE
RUNNING ON 8 DRIVING WHEELS, 4' DIAM. ALL
CONNECTED

BOILER ARRANGED TO BURN ANTHRACITE
COAL; BUILT AT THE BORDENTOWN SHOPS
1836.
Scale 1" = 1 ft.

crown sheet held up by
crow feet stays

Figure 28. An engraving of the *Monster* based on an original drawing. The steamdome and the firedoor indicate that the boiler pictured here is the rebuilt version. (*Locomotive Engineering*, February 1890.)

was intended to be purely a coal burner. Her failure to do so was a disappointment, but she did develop enough steam on one occasion to burst the riveted seams around the steam-dome and send that portion of the boiler high into the heavens. This unplanned event did, however, present an occasion to remodel the boiler along more efficient lines.[13] Dripps replaced the steamdome, but he also added a small firedoor and a set of grates to the combustion chamber, making it a second firebox. The grates of the principal fire-box were raised about midway in the box. A multiple-jet blastpipe was added to the smokebox, and the smokestack was made to taper from its bottom to its top opening. To further enliven the fire, a blower, driven by a small oscillating steam engine, was mounted on top of the boiler. The fan created a better draft and thus stimulated the fire. The *Monster* as reformed became a moderately good steam producer. The independent cut-off valve gear (partially outlined in fig. 28) helped conserve steam and is one of the earliest recorded instances of the use of such a device. The *Monster* received major repairs in 1850 and continued in service until the early 1860s. It was last used as a switcher at South Amboy before being condemned and cut up.

Logic would dictate the creation of only one *Monster* as a noble experiment. Yet seemingly other considerations directed motive-power policy on the C&A. In 1852 and 1854 the line acquired five more *Monster*-class freight locomotives. Nos. 33, 34, 42, and 43 were built by the Trenton Locomotive and Machine Company, No. 35 was produced at Bordentown. All five had eight 48-inch-diameter driving wheels and 18-by-30-inch cylinders. The first three weighed 33 tons, while the last two registered 35 tons on the scales. While considerably larger than the original No.

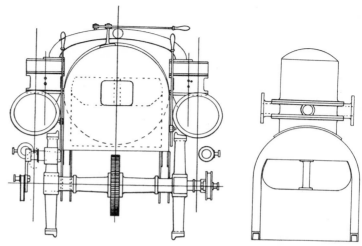

Figure 29. Cross sections of the *Monster*. (*Locomotive Engineering*, February 1890.)

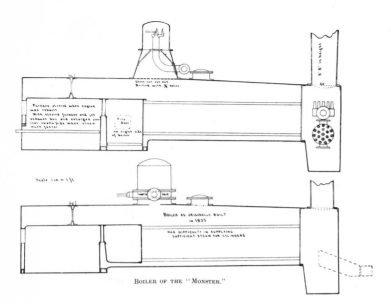

Scale 1 in = 1 ft.

BOILER OF THE "MONSTER."

Figure 30. *Top:* The *Monster's* boiler as originally built. *Bottom:* The boiler as rebuilt after the steamdome blew off. (*Locomotive Engineering,* February 1890.)

17, the latter-day versions shared the design peculiarities of their prototype—the pendulum drive and the wheel-axle pedestals riveted to the boiler. One new feature, a hot-water heater, was introduced.[14] The ashpan was made with a double bottom to form a tank three inches deep. The feedwater was pumped from the ashpan to the smokebox for additional heating before being injected into the boiler. A local newspaper, the *Trenton American,* went on to note that the boiler was 24 feet long and 50 inches in diameter. The firebox was very large for that period and measured 47 inches wide by 84 inches long. The engine was rated at 350 horsepower.

Not long after the first of the new *Monsters* were delivered, Isaac Dripps left the employ of the C&A to become a partner in the Trenton Locomotive and Machine Company. His successor, Samuel B. Dougherty, tried to salvage something from the misguided investment of his predecessor by rebuilding the Monster class along more conventional lines. Presumably this work was done in the 1860s. The original *Monster,* too small and now obsolete, was retired as already mentioned, but its newer sisters were remodeled as 4-6-0's. A four-wheel leading truck replaced the front pair of driving wheels. Link motion succeeded the complex cutoff-valve gear. However, budget constraints discouraged Dougherty from a more complete reordering of Dripps's pet design, and so the inclined cylinders and pendulum-arm drive were retained. The result was a mechanical creature of the most unlikely and bizarre appearance (fig. 31). A few of these curiosities remained in service until about 1875.[15]

Before the last of the *Monsters* were placed in service, the C&A motive-power department went off on another tangent. This time the passenger side of the business was in-

Figure 31. One of the second-generation Monsters as remodeled from a geared 0-8-0 to a rod-powered 4-6-0 by S. B. Dougherty in about 1865. The original No. 35 was produced by the Bordentown shops. (*Locomotive Engineering*, February 1890.)

Figure 32. This lithograph was issued by Norris Brothers some months before the *John Stevens* was delivered and appears to vary in several details from the actual machine as it was produced. Note the extremely heavy rail depicted in the track. (Smithsonian Neg. 41,139.)

volved in the most recent innovation in locomotive design to attract Robert Stevens's fancy. The railroad had acquired several standard eight-wheelers from Baldwin, Norris, and Newcastle during the 1840s, but these conventional machines did little to excite Stevens's admiration. That they were able to reliably move trains over the line seems to have made little impression. Stevens was again restless and in pursuit of a more novel form of passenger locomotive. His opportunity came late in 1846 when he resigned as president of the C&A Railroad and made an extended tour of Europe. While in England he was introduced to an extraordinary design for high-speed locomotives patented by Thomas R. Crampton in 1842. Crampton proposed a high-wheel locomotive, with a single pair of driving wheels at the rear, a leading truck, and a very low-slung boiler. It was his idea to combine speed and safety in a single machine. He believed a major defect of express passenger locomotives was their high center of gravity. The trade press was excited by Crampton's bold plan and gave it considerable coverage. Even the *American Railroad Journal* published some articles and an engraving.[16] Industry leaders in general were less enthusiastic, and no Crampton engines were built for actual service until the year of Stevens's tour. The first Cramptons were built in England for use in Belgium. Stevens was apparently captivated by the novelty of the design and returned to New Jersey determined to stock the C&A with high wheelers on this plan.

From the outset it is easy to criticize Stevens's advocacy of any form of express locomotive for use on the Camden and Amboy. While it was one of the better-built pioneer American railroads, it was in no way suitable for high-speed trains. It was relatively straight and level, but it was

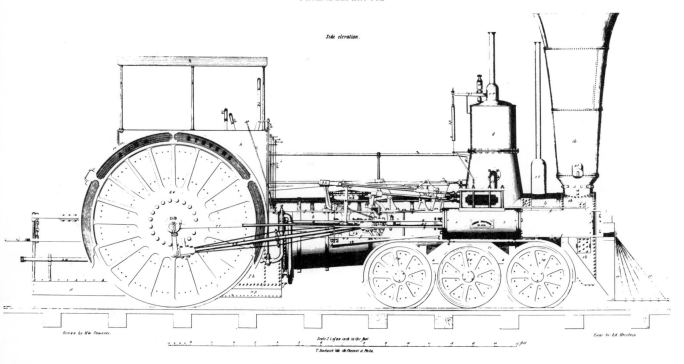

Figure 33. Side elevation of the *John Stevens*, a high-speed passenger locomotive equipped with 96-inch drivers. The drawing was published in Emil Reuter's *American Locomotives* in 1849. (Courtesy of the Library of Congress.)

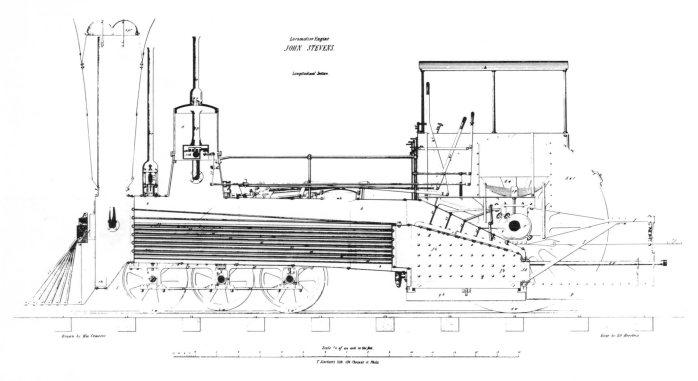

Figure 34. Longitudinal cross section of the *John Stevens*, from Reuter's book of 1849. Note the low level of the fireman's deck to the rear of the firebox. (Courtesy of the Library of Congress.)

single tracked and had light wrought-iron rail, some of which was set on stone block ties. It had no block signaling. Even telegraphic train orders were in the future. Its trains, quite sensibly, averaged little better than twenty or twenty-five miles an hour. No one knew these conditions better than Stevens. One can only assume that he dreamed of a superrailroad as part of a vision for high-speed service between New York and Philadelphia. There is some evidence to support this speculation, namely, the 92-pound rail that the Camden and Amboy tested in 1848–49. The experiment ultimately failed, and whatever support Stevens may have garnered from the other directors of the railroad diminished rather quickly. The superrailroad was never built in Stevens's lifetime; however, before the failure of the high rail was proved or the staggering cost of rebuilding the railroad for high-speed service was fully documented, he did win authority to proceed with the purchase of Crampton-style engines. In 1847 Dripps set to work at the drafting table. The resulting drawings might even have nonplussed Thomas Crampton, for the machine pictured was a wondrously complex assemblage that seemed to be all bars, rods, levers, and spokes. One is tempted to name it the ugliest locomotive ever built for main-line service, yet to be kinder, perhaps we should say that it was designed with emphasis on utility rather than beauty (fig. 33).

The drawings were turned over to Norris Brothers of Philadelphia, then the largest commercial locomotive builders in the United States. In April 1849 they had the No. 28—named *John Stevens* in honor of R. L. Stevens's father—ready for testing. The cylinders had an unusually long stroke of 34 inches and a relatively small bore of 13 inches. But of course few observers would pay much atten-

tion to the cylinders, which were visually overwhelmed by the fantastic 8-foot drivers, the towering spark arrester, and the six-wheel leading truck. To hold down boiler weight, only 3/16-inch-thick sheets were used. Total weight of the engine in working order was estimated at 22 tons; only 8.25 tons were on the drivers.[17] This engine is unusually well documented. Norris Brothers published a lithograph of it before delivery that depicts what is presumably a modified study design since it does not agree with later pictorial documents (fig. 32). The lithograph, dated 1848, shows a headlight, an arched window cab, a capped stack, and other features that do not agree with published working drawings. The drawings were included in a folio book by Emil Reuter entitled *American Locomotives* (Philadelphia, 1849) and are reproduced here (figs. 33–36). A photograph taken not long after the No. 28 entered service confirms that the engine was made in accordance with the plans published in Reuter's book (fig. 37). Many years later, specifications taken from the Norris order books, since lost, were published in the February 1889 issue of *Locomotive Engineering*:

One passenger Loco. for Camden & Amboy Ry. Gauge 4′ 9⅞″.

Boiler. 38 inches diam., made with spiral seams to burn anthracite coal, the steam dome to be put on cyl. part of boiler, with steam pipes leading to steam chests.

Cylinders. 13x34 inches. Horizontal.

Cut Off. Worked from an eccentric on outside of shackle pin.

Guides. Of steel, with block and heads.

Crossheads. Of wrought-iron, with cylindrical journals.

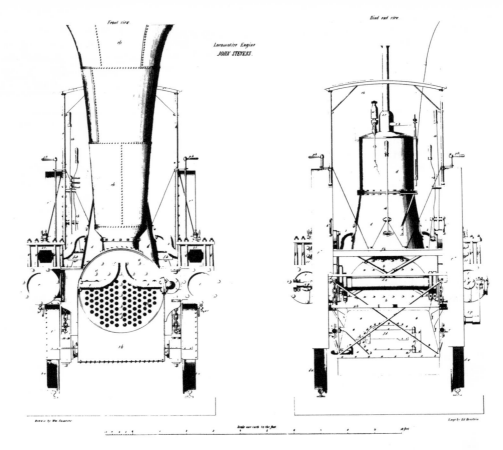

Figure 35. Front and rear elevations of the *John Stevens*, from Reuter's book. (Courtesy of the Library of Congress.)

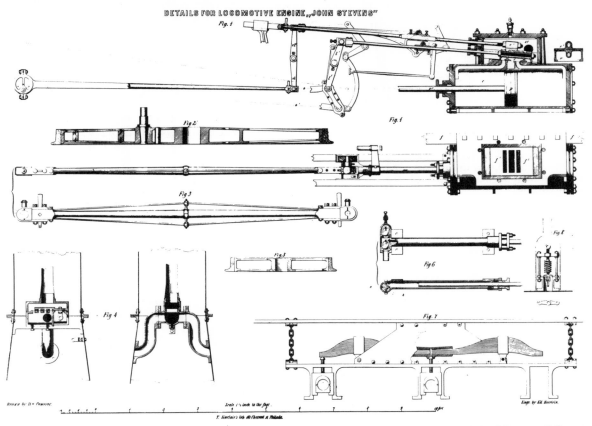

Figure 36. Valve gear and other details of the *John Stevens*, shown in Reuter's book. (Courtesy of the Library of Congress.)

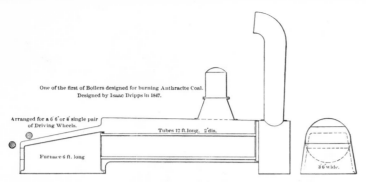

Figure 38. A boiler study drawing prepared in 1847 by Isaac Dripps. According to an old employee, the elbow stack was actually used on at least one engine. (*Master Mechanics Report,* 1884.)

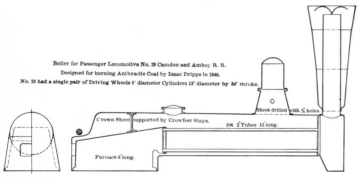

Figure 39. A second boiler study drawing prepared by Isaac Dripps in 1848, intended for use on the Crampton-style engines. (*Master Mechanics Report,* 1884.)

Wheels. 2 driving wheels, 8 feet dia.

Axles. Axle 6¾, truck wheels with tires 36″ dia. Axles 4″ dia.

Tubes. 98, of iron, 2″ dia., 12′ long.

Name, John Stevens, No. 28, tried April 17, 1849.

Just a few years before this data was committed to print, Isaac Dripps furnished copies of several early locomotive-boiler drawings to the American Railway Master Mechanics Association, all of which were reproduced in their 1884 and 1885 annual reports. Two of these drawings were apparently studies for the No. 28 (figs. 38 and 39). Both drawings show certain features that were not incorporated in the locomotive as built. The curious elbow smokestack shown in one drawing is worthy of notice. It was made so that it could be turned out of the wind from the cab by a system of rods. One account claims that the plan was actually used on one of the Cramptons.[18]

Despite the planning and high expectations, the No. 28's performance fell short of Dripps's expectations. He was discouraged by the engine's low tractive effort and the resulting difficulty in starting even light passenger trains. This defect could easily be traced to too little weight on the drivers, only one pair of driving wheels, and oversized cylinders. The boiler was not particularly proficient in producing steam, even with its large firebox, because of the slow-burning anthracite coal used as fuel.[19] However, once the train was under way the slippery 96-inch wheels would take hold, and one old employee declared "they would run as fast as men cared to ride"; perhaps even faster than some men cared to ride.

Stevens did not share Dripps's disaffection for the No. 28

Figure 37. A photograph of the *John Stevens*. Note how closely it conforms to the drawings in the previous illustrations.

Figure 41. One of the earliest photographs of an American locomotive. The No. 30 was built by Norris Brothers in 1850. (Smithsonian Neg. 77-9035.)

and ordered four more Cramptons from Norris Brothers. It was apparently believed that a longer stroke would improve the starting power of the engines, because the new engines were fitted with 13-by-38-inch cylinders. (Actually a larger bore and shorter stroke would have been more efficient.) Nos. 29–32 differed from their sisters in a few other details. The steamdome was set back more toward the center of the boiler. The smokebox was moved forward and was not cut away to clear the front pair of leading wheels. The wooden frame was placed on an angle to meet the pilot beam. The valve gear, at least on the No. 30, was driven by a crank minus the eccentric used on the No. 28. The openings between the spokes were made solid with the insertion of thin wooden panels. This was done to assist in keeping the engines clean, because the giant wheels acted as tremendous fans in stirring up dust as they roared along the tracks. The wheels were cast iron and made after a plan worked out by Dripps in June 1848 (fig. 40).[20] It was claimed that wrought-iron wheel centers imported from England had failed in service, and yet the supposedly weaker cast-iron wheels designed by Dripps never cracked a single spoke in all their running years.

Two remarkably clear photographs of one of the new Cramptons, the No. 30, have survived. They are among the very oldest American locomotive photographs to survive and are also most assuredly the best prints we have from this early date. One of them can definitely be ascribed to the famous photographers F. and W. Langenheim of Philadelphia. The original print of the side view (fig. 41) is now in the Smithsonian's Division of Photography. The print was made from a calotype or paper negative. (This ancient print was so badly faded that the image was barely discernible. It

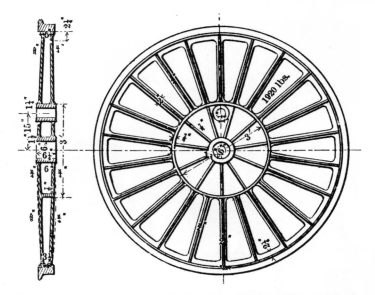

Figure 40. Dripps's plan for a 96-inch-diameter cast-iron driving wheel was made June 14, 1848. (*Locomotive Engineering*, July 1889.)

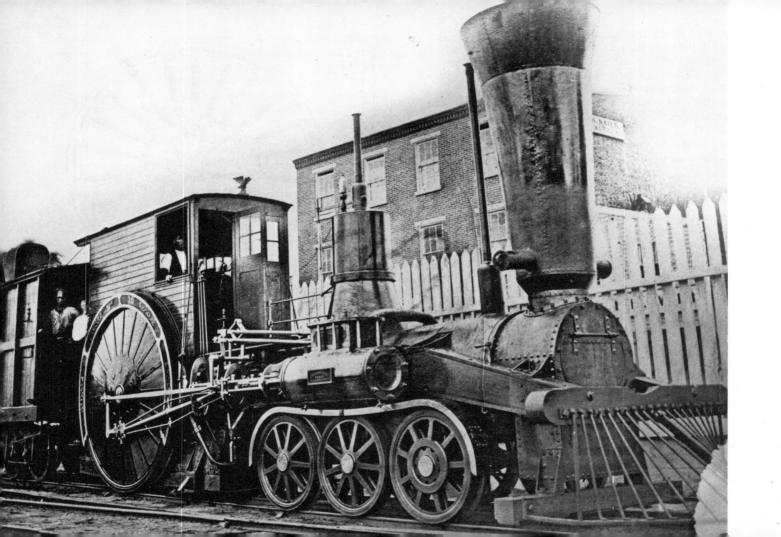

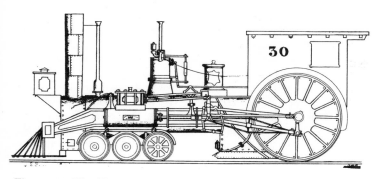

Figure 43. The No. 30 late in its career, as sketched by J. Snowden Bell in 1860.

Figure 42. The Camden and Amboy's No. 30 is portrayed in this remarkable photograph believed to have been made in 1850. (Chaney Neg. 2455.)

was miraculously restored in recent years through the expertise of the Smithsonian's curator of photography, Eugene Ostroff.) The front three-quarter view is presumably the work of the same photographers; however, only photographic copies made at a later period are known to have survived into modern times. It is worth comparing a pencil sketch made by J. Snowden Bell in 1860 of the No. 30 (fig. 43) with the two aforementioned photographs to perceive the alterations made over one decade. Note the addition of a headlight and sandbox, together with the straight smokestack and solid-plate leading wheels.

The first of the new Cramptons, the No. 29, was delivered in the spring of 1850. It had only been in service a short time when the boiler exploded with disastrous results near Bordentown.[21] Low water was blamed for the failure that killed four crew members and all but destroyed the road's latest roster addition. James White, an apprentice at the Bordentown shops at the time of the accident, was sent out with the wrecking crew to clear the line. The engine was blown across the tracks, about 300 feet from the point at which it exploded. White explained what happened to the crew:

The engineer, Martin Dale Fisher, fell some fifty feet up the line, beyond the locomotive, landing on his feet on the south side of a cow pit, which ran under the railroad. His body rebounded over the pit falling on his head. A Mr. Field, who was standing near, ran to him and found him dead. Mr. Seward, who was riding with Mr. Fisher was found dead on the engine where it fell. The first fireman, Mr. Henry, escaped with slight injury. The second fireman, E. Greenleaf, was standing in front of the furnace door at the time, and as the end of the boiler blew out, pieces of the half burnt coal were forced into his face and body. He survived until the following morning when he died, as did the top brakeman who was scalded.

After this disaster, the railroad decided to make its own inspection of the No. 29's sisters as they arrived from the Norris plant. The No. 30 failed a hydrostatic test in a most frightening fashion. At 150 pounds, the firebox stays began to give way with reports sounding like a muffled gun discharging. Next the front firebox sheet burst its entire width. What measures were taken to remedy these defects are not recorded, but one can imagine the uneasy feelings of the men who mounted the footplates above the burbling firebox of the No. 30 and her sisters over the next decade or so that they remained in service.

Because failure was never to be admitted by Robert Stevens, two more Cramptons were procured from Messrs. Norris in April 1853. Nos. 37 and 38 differed somewhat from their predecessors. Both had 14-by-38-inch cylinders. The No. 37 was constructed as a wood burner, while the No. 38 had a straight outer wrapper over the firebox and a central combustion chamber. Dripps, ever innovative, placed deflecting plates in the smokebox, added a high-exhaust nozzle, and, to prevent priming, placed a dished plate under the throttle-valve opening. Yet these features, considered very advanced for the time, together with all the prayers and stubborn optimism of their creator, could not make the Cramptons a success. That they ran very much as designed for over ten years is a miracle. But both Stevens and Dripps were gone by 1856, and less emotionally involved men were now the masters. They saw little to champion or applaud. Late in 1856 one of the Cramptons, proba-bly No. 37 (the wood burner), was rebuilt as a 4-4-0.[22] Six-foot-diameter drivers were placed on 6-foot centers; the four-wheel leading truck had a 5-foot spread. Link motion replaced the complex independent cutoff-valve gear, and the central combustion chamber was removed. The old long-stroke cylinders were retained. More rebuildings followed, but at a measured pace. The No. 31 was depicted and described very much in its original form in March 1862 (fig. 45).[23] The following dimensions were offered at the time of the report: the boiler was 36 inches in diameter and contained 73 flues, 11 feet 2 inches long by 2 inches in diameter. The steamdome stood 56 inches high. The connecting rods measured 8 feet 8 inches long. The driving axle was 7 inches in diameter. The distance from the center of the truck to the center of the driving wheels was 14 feet 6 inches. The truck wheels were 28 inches in diameter. The No. 31 was soon remodeled, and so another curiosity left over from the Stevens administration vanished. As late as November 1865 one of the engineering magazines briefly mentioned the rebuilding of one of the old Cramptons along conventional lines, thus marking the end of this misadventure in American locomotive design.

The new motive-power chief, Samuel B. Dougherty, had clearly decided to join the mainstream of American locomotive practice. The aging and undersized 2-2-2-0's were retired or sold. The Monsters and Cramptons were remodeled along more familiar lines. Dougherty also began to purchase or build a fleet of modern 4-4-0's and 4-6-0's. Between roughly 1858 and 1865 he succeeded in restocking the line. Most of the purchased power came from Danforth, Cooke, and Company in Paterson, New Jersey, but a goodly portion of the new engines were homemade. Fortunately a

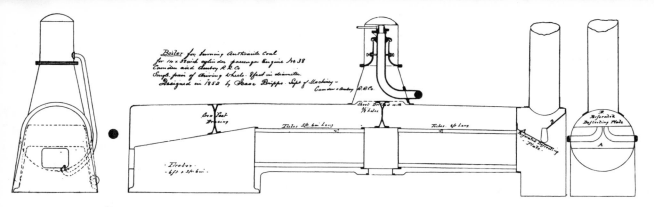

Figure 44. The boiler for Crampton No. 38 was drawn by Isaac Dripps in 1852. The engine was delivered in the following year by Norris Brothers. (*Master Mechanics Report*, 1885.)

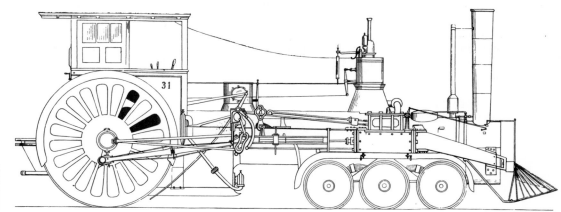

Figure 45. The No. 31 as it last appeared before being remodeled into an eight wheeler. (*American Railway Review*, March 6, 1862.)

Figure 46. The road number for this C&A veteran has not been determined. It may be one of the remodeled Cramptons, but if so, small new cylinders have been added. (Chaney Neg. 3094.)

Figure 47. Samuel B. Dougherty (1812–1893) succeeded Isaac Dripps as the C&A's master mechanic and proceeded to restock the line with more conventional locomotives. (New York Central Photo 6005.)

few photographs of the latter have been preserved, and they show that some of the uniqueness of the old times was carried over (figs. 49 and 50). In both photographs of the new Nos. 18 and 63 are seen distinctive features that alert the expert eye that the machines were not ordinary products of a commercial builder. The outside mounting of the link motion is the most obvious telltale. Note the outside bearing truck of the No. 63—this is not unique to the C&A, but it is unusual. The H-pattern spoked driving wheels are probably the exclusive hallmark of the C&A, at least at this late date. Notice that the drivers on the No. 18 are fitted with wooden panels just like those used on the Cramptons. The bell stand on both engines is uniform and bears a remarkable similarity to those used by Cooke during this period. Perhaps they were even supplied by the Paterson maker. It should also be noted that Dougherty remained loyal to the old-fashioned box tender that dated back to the beginnings of the C&A. From the photographic evidence available, even the engines supplied by commercial builders had tenders of this type. Their advantages over the conventional U-tank design are questionable. The enclosed fuel space must have made loading of either coal or wood difficult. The large vertical water tank would not help lower the center of gravity. And no one could argue that the design was attractive or pleasing in its proportions.

In 1867 Dougherty built four large ten-wheelers for freight service at Bordentown. They were the largest engines on the line and were rated to haul one-hundred-car freight trains.[24] Dougherty continued to build new engines at the company shops even after the Pennsylvania lease took effect. But not many months had passed before the new owners let it be known that only standard PRR-class

Figure 48. Cooke supplied the new No. 4 in 1859. Note the characteristic enclosed tender so long favored on the C&A Railroad. (Chaney Neg. 5429.)

Figure 49. The Bordentown shops built the No. 18, a coal burner, in 1866. (Courtesy of the DeGolyer Foundation Library.)

engines would henceforth be satisfactory, and these could more economically be produced at the great Altoona works in central Pennsylvania. Dougherty was accordingly let go, and the Bordentown shops were closed about 1874.[25].

In the summer of 1881 a new firm was organized to re-open the old shops, presumably for new locomotive construction. A lease was effected with the PRR, and Dougherty was named superintendent.[26] The scheme must have faltered, for a few years later it was announced that the four-acre facility was being rented by Albert H. King, who planned to stock and repair secondhand locomotives and cars.[27] Bordentown shops—once the prestigious home of some of the most advanced and unique steam locomotives in North America—had come full circle. Bordentown was now a weed-grown graveyard filled with rusty derelicts and forlorn junkers awaiting their last assignment on some obscure short line far removed from the humming main line, just across the Delaware River, that connected the greatest cities in North America. Time, men, and machines had simply passed by Bordentown.

Notes

1. Data from order books of Robert Stephenson and Company, Science Musuem, London.

2. Franz A.R. Von Gerstner, *Die Innern Communication der Vereinigten Staaten von Nord Amerika* (Vienna, 1842–43), 2:87.

3. Jonathan Knight and B.H. Latrobe, *Report Upon the Locomotive Engines . . . Several of the Principal Rail Roads in the Northern and Middle States* (Baltimore, 1838), p. 27.

4. *American Railroad Journal*, 29 June 1833, p. 405.

5. *National Cyclopedia of American Biography* 24:359; *Louisiana Planter and Sugar Manufacturing*, 7 Feb. 1914, p. 93.

6. John H. White, Jr., *American Locomotives, 1830–1880: An Engineering History* (Baltimore, 1968), p. 280.

7. *Railway Review*, 20 Oct. 1883, p. 614.

8. *American Railway Review*, 8 May 1862, p. 67.

9. *Perth Amboy Evening News*, 21 Sept. 1906. James White wrote a long letter to the editors recounting his experiences and recollections as a C&A employee between 1846 and 1900. For most of these years White served as a locomotive engineer. (Hereafter "White's Recollections.")

10. *Locomotive Engineering*, Feb. 1890, pp. 20–23. Claims work started in 1833, which appears too early, considering that the boiler drawing is dated 1835 and the machine was not completed until about 1838.

11. "White's Recollections."

12. Minute book of the Camden and Amboy Railroad, formerly in the possession of the secretary of the Pennsylvania Railroad.

13. *Master Mechanics Report* (1885), pp. 48–49, reproduces a letter from Isaac Dripps explaining the rebuilding of the *Monster.*

14. Quotations from *Trenton American* appear in *Farmer and Mechanic*, 28 Aug. 1852, p. 429.

15. *Locomotive Engineering*, Feb. 1890, p. 23.

16. *American Railroad Journal*, 1846, p. 296; ibid., 1847, pp. 262, 293, and 325.

17. Z. Colburn, *Locomotive Engineering and the Mechanism of Railways* (London, 1871 and 1872), p. 72.

18. *Locomotive Engineering*, Feb. 1889, p. 1.

19. *Railroad Gazette,* 15 Aug. 1879, p. 435.

20. *Locomotive Engineering*, July 1889, p. 4.

21. *American Railroad Journal*, 9 Mar. 1850, p. 153; "White's Recollections."

22. *Railroad Advocate*, 25 Apr. 1857, p. 8, reports the rebuilding of a Crampton a few months previously.

23. *American Railway Review*, 6 Mar. 1862, p. 343.

24. *Journal of the Franklin Institute*, June 1867, p. 367.

25. *Railway Age*, 1 Sept. 1881, p. 499.

26. *Railroad Gazette*, 8 July 1881, p. 378; ibid., 19 Aug. 1881, p. 353.

27. *Railway Review*, 17 Nov. 1888, p. 666.

BUILT AT THE C. & A. R. R. CO.'S SHOPS,

PHOTOGRAPHED BY SEXTON & TANTUM.

BORDENTOWN, N. J.

Figure 50. Another Bordentown product of the 1860s. The proud gent leaning on the pilot beam is believed to be S. B. Dougherty. (Chaney Neg. 3108.)

Figure 51. Even after the introduction of bridges and improved roads, the fastest road coach required nearly two days to make the journey between New York and Philadelphia.

III. The Camden and Amboy Railroad

During the earliest period of European settlement in what is now the northeastern United States, there was little intercourse between the Dutch, English, and Swedish encampments. The colonials were isolated from one another by forests and a largely hostile native population, as well as national and religious differences. By 1700, however, the area was politically united. New Amsterdam and New Sweden were swallowed up as part of British North America. The once fragile and temporary fortifications were becoming lively centers of trade. A few places, like New York and Philadelphia, were clearly destined to become cities. At the same time, Native Americans were withdrawing from the coastline. Limited travel began between the various colonial settlements in the area.

In theory, the constraints that discouraged travel were now removed. But in the practical sense, very real physical barriers remained stubbornly in place. How could one travel when roads, bridges, docks, and ferries were so rare? Coastal vessels offered a path around overland barriers, but water routes were indirect and often dangerous. New Jersey was most inconveniently placed and blocked a direct water passage between Philadelphia and New York. The Delaware River was equally inconsiderate: if only it would empty into New York Harbor rather than turn south to the Chésapeake Bay. Storms, fogs, and headwinds made sailing a sickening, risky, and uncertain mode of travel. Most commercial travelers were businessmen, not sailors, and their time, to say nothing of their personal safety, was very precious to them. Cautious men sought an overland route for at least part of the journey. This could be accomplished by hiring a carriage to traverse the pathways hacked through the woodlands of New Jersey that separated lower New

York Harbor from the Delaware River.

To speak only in general about the hardships of travel is an abstraction that can best be brought to life by the experience of a single individual. In 1723 young Ben Franklin made his way between New York and Philadelphia. The journey, as recalled in his autobiography, was a disaster from the outset. A storm drove his boat away from New Jersey to the Long Island shore; after thirty hours on rough seas, the sturdy craft finally worked its way back to Amboy. The storm followed Franklin overland so that he was continuously drenched by the rain. He made his sodden way to the Delaware River only to miss the biweekly boat. Rather than wait, he rented a small boat and rowed himself to Philadelphia. This miserable experience encompassed all of six days.

By 1733 the traffic along Franklin's route had become so well established that a weekly stage wagon began operations between Amboy and Burlington. Within a few years a boat began operations between Bordentown and Philadelphia on the Delaware River, and if the demand was really heavy, two stage wagons would be operated during a single week. Even so, the entire trip took four to five days and was suspended during the spring and winter because of poor road conditions. Better roads encouraged travelers to go via Newark and Bergen (now Jersey City) in 1766, when stagecoaches under the best weather conditions could complete the journey between Philadelphia and New York in only two days. This miracle was made possible by improved roads and new stage wagons referred to as "Flying Machines." Within a short time, year-round service was offered by six stages on a weekly basis. The inland route was improved in post-Revolution years by the construction of large bridges over the Passaic, Hackensack, and Delaware rivers, thus ending the delays caused by floods and ice at these crossings. The wooden, five-arch span over the Delaware River, which opened at Trenton in 1806, was considered an engineering triumph (fig. 52). Such improvements trimmed another twelve hours off the stagecoach schedules.

The emergence of commercial steam boating about 1810 shifted some of the traffic back to the original water-land-water route. The steamers were fast, reasonably safe, and independent of the tide and wind. Passengers could board one of the Stevens family Union Line sidewheelers on the south end of Manhattan and steam over to South Amboy. A stage would then deliver them to a riverboat at Bordentown, which in turn deposited them at the ferry dock in Philadelphia. Some passengers preferred the rival route that involved a ferry ride to Jersey City, a stage to Trenton, and a riverboat ride to Philadelphia. The complicated bookings for either route were annoying, and so in 1823 the Stevens family offered consolidated ticketing via their South Amboy route. They controlled and operated the boats and the stages. Luggage could be checked through, thus relieving the traveler of this most troublesome feature of the journey.* Not long after the introduction of through

---

* After the railroad opened, luggage was placed in large boxes or crates mounted on wheels, which could be readily transferred between the flatcars and the lower deck of the steamboat or ferry. These boxes, antecedents of the modern container, facilitated the shipment of baggage and small parcels over the land-sea route of the Camden and Amboy line. The containers were covered to protect their contents. Each was labeled, some going through the en-

ticketing, one could expect to move from Wall Street to Market Street via steamer, stage, and ferry in ten to eleven hours. To those who could remember when it took days and not hours to make the same journey, the age of steam was indeed an age of wonders.

There were even more wonders in the offing. The very same men who had done so much to improve water travel were now ready to apply steam to land transport. Even before 1812, old John Stevens had proposed steam railroads for the area. Now his sons were busy with plans to make his vision a reality. By the late 1820s, the number of passengers traveling between New York and Philadelphia had grown to some 2,000 a week. Figuring an average of four dollars per passenger, gross annual revenues brought in more than $400,000—a vast sum of money in the gold-standard days. There was an economic stimulus to capture this market by effecting an unrivaled system of transport, and this the Stevens brothers hoped to do by building a railroad over the shortest possible portage route. This line would connect the fast steamers they were already operating.

Meetings with local citizens to promote support for the project started in January of 1828. Petitions for a charter were presented to the state legislature, but no majority

Figure 52. The giant wooden arch bridge over the Delaware River at Trenton was designed and built by Theodore Burr in 1804–06. It was later used by the Philadelphia and Trenton Railroad. (J. W. Barber and Henry Howe, *Historical Collections of New Jersey,* 1844.)

tire journey while others were dropped off at predetermined points. In this way the train was not delayed while baggage clerks sorted out bags and express; instead, the head-end train crew would roll the container off the baggage car to the station platform. The local agent would distribute the luggage after the train departed. Empty containers were returned to the ferry stations on a following train.

Figure 53. Robert L. Stevens (1787–1856)
was president and chief engineer of the
Camden and Amboy Railroad and Transportation Company.
(Angus Sinclair, *Development of the Locomotive Engine,* 1907.)

could be raised at first to support the scheme within that body. The know-nothing prejudice that greeted John Stevens's plan of 1811 had subsided—one newspaper editor had even admitted he did not know what a railroad was but was nevertheless firmly opposed to its introduction. This kind of thinking was no longer articulated, but clearly the railroad notion was unfamiliar to the average citizen. It was opposed by stage and tavern operators who were not enamored with the prospect of becoming victims of evolution. At this juncture Robert F. Stockton (1795–1866), a prominent figure in the political and financial affairs of New Jersey, guided the railroad project through the legislative labyrinth. As part of the inevitable compromise, a charter was granted on February 4, 1830, to the railroad *and* to a rival canal, the Delaware and Raritan, of which Stockton happened to be president. The railroad was granted a one-hundred-foot-wide right-of-way. Work was to begin within two years and was to be completed in no less than nine years from the date of the charter. Capital was fixed at $1 million, but it could be increased by 50 percent if so desired. A tax or transit duty was to be paid to the state on all passengers and goods hauled. This would end if the state chartered a line across New Jersey that terminated within three miles of the C&A. The state retained the option to buy the property at fair value when the charter expired in 1860. Stockton remained a shareholder and a loyal friend of the newly formed Camden and Amboy Railroad and Transportation Company throughout his life. And he was in a position to render good service to his corporate friend both within and without the state capitol building. The Stevens family was also influential and they, together with such powerful friends as Stockton, succeeded in obtaining more favorable treatment, as will be explained in the following pages.

With the charter now granted, the Camden and Amboy was organized on April 28 with Robert L. Stevens as president and chief engineer and Edwin A. Stevens as treasurer. With the enterprise in such prestigious hands, all skepticism evaporated. The entire capital stock of the company was fully subscribed on the first day the books were opened—$1 million was paid in. By contrast the R&D Canal had waited a full year to sell its shares. Investors were clearly betting on the iron horse. A survey party, headed by Major John Wilson, took to the field and completed its reconnaissance by October 1830. Stevens then sailed for England to procure a locomotive and rails. Construction reportedly began in December. This seems rather premature, for not only had winter set in—hardly a favorable season for outdoor civil-engineering work—but no rail was delivered until August of the following year. It is possible that some preliminary grading was done at this time, perhaps as a show to reassure the shareholders that the project was actually under way.

Though construction was just starting, the managers of the fledgling line were already obsessed with fears about the building of rival lines that might siphon off part of their traffic. Other railroad charters were being granted, with many more pending. The C&A wanted more security than that offered in its original thirty-year charter, and so it returned to the state capital. Its efforts were rewarded with a remarkable piece of legislation passed in February 1831 that is sometimes known as the Marriage Act. It allowed for a partial consolidation of the C&A Railroad and the D&R Canal. It also extended the corporate life of the ca-

nal for another twenty years. The capital stock of both was combined, yet each would have its own offices, directors, and cash books. The boards would meet jointly and be presided over by a joint chairman elected for the purpose. The Joint Companies, as they were afterwards known, agreed to pay the state a transit duty of ten cents for each passenger carried over the line and fifteen cents for each ton of goods carried. As with all taxes, it was the public and not the corporation which paid the extra levees. Passenger rates were ten cents a mile, and freight rates were not to go beyond eight cents per ton mile. Because both rates were extremely high, the public's interest was hardly being protected. The Joint Companies gave the state 1,000 shares of nonvoting stock valued at $100 per share at the time of charter. It now agreed to pay no less than $30,000 to the state per annum in transit duties. The Joint Companies also offered the state government another 1,000 shares if their monopoly was made more secure. Some legislators saw this offer as a bonanza that would greatly reduce the need for unpopular local taxes. They passed a bill on March 2, 1832, which more firmly established the railroad monopoly on all traffic across New Jersey between New York and Philadelphia. It was stipulated that no rail line could be built across New Jersey between New York and Philadelphia without the consent of the Joint Companies. Gone were the subtle threats about merely ending payment of the transit duties. The C&A now had ironclad protection against any rival railroad. This extraordinary measure was a flagrant restraint upon interstate trade that became one of the hottest issues in state politics, yet it somehow stood despite the bitterest protests of the antimonopolists. The inability of a competitor to obtain a charter guaranteed a vastly profitable traffic to the Joint Companies. Just how golden that harvest proved to be was well documented over the ensuing decades.

News of the railroad's construction was less clamorous and more sparsely reported than the cloakroom maneuverings just recounted. Work appears to have made little progress until the fall of 1832. On September 19 the first section of line opened between Bordentown and Hightstown. The fourteen-mile trip was made with horse-drawn cars. Passengers were carried by road coach to Hightstown. By mid-December of the same year the single-track line reached South Amboy. A deep cut necessary to carry the tracks to the steamer landing delayed construction for some time. A picture of travel on the Camden and Amboy was published in the May 4, 1833, *American Railroad Journal:*

> We have recently journeyed between Philadelphia and New York by the railroad line. Yesterday we left New York in the beautiful and spacious boat the New Philadelphia, at about a quarter past six o'clock, A.M., and arrived at Chestnut street wharf before three P.M. The New Philadelphia reached South Amboy in two hours and a quarter. The fine and commodious cars on the railroad were drawn to Bordentown eleven miles the hour, without undue fatigue of the horses, or any circumstance that could lessen the sense of security and comfort with which every passenger seems to set out.
>
> This conveyance is truly admirable for the ease and order which attend it for all parties. Each car is divided into three compartments, and contains twenty-four persons. Two horses are attached to it *tandem;* they pursue the track, under the guidance of skilful drivers, with the nicest exactness. We could not perceive, by the motion of the vehicle, the slightest deviation from the grooves; and the

> route is of more than 30 miles. One track is complete: great activity prevails in the work necessary for the accomplishment of the whole design. The average duration of the journey between the two great cities, by this railroad line, is now eight or eight and a half hours. It will be less, considerably, when a locomotive engine shall be employed. A new and spacious steamboat is also to be soon provided. We shall then see the consummation of all that can be deemed desirable, for we presume that such precautions can be taken as would exclude almost the possibility of serious accidents or delays.
>
> At present breakfast may be taken at home, and an invitation to dinner at New York or Philadelphia for 3 o'clock, accepted with the assurance of a timely arrival. Ere very long, we may presume, the journey between Baltimore and New York will be performed in the summer in one day by the light of the sun; and this without weariness from motion. In the same way the Philadelphian may visit New York and return by the family tea-hour. The facilities which this railroad provides for the transportation of merchandise, provisions, and so forth, form another signal advantage, upon which we might descant in greater detail; but they are readily to be conceived and appreciated. Experience will teach their value before the next autumn.

Three changes of horses, two per car, were made en route. The September 14, 1833, *American Railroad Journal* noted that 180 horses were employed in this service. Horse-drawn freight cars began running in January of 1833; however, the horse-car days were soon to end as more locomotives were readied for service. Steam operations began in September 1833. A Newark paper excitedly reported that locomotives whirled six- or seven-car trains over the line at

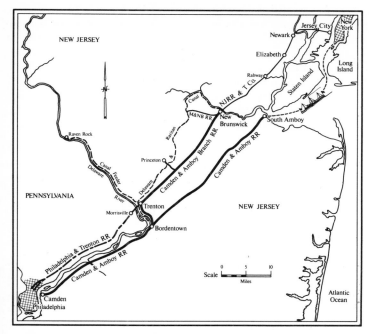

Figure 54. The Camden and Amboy and its connections. (Drawing by Elizabeth Tone Summers.)

speeds up to thirty miles an hour. One engine was derailed by a hog. There would have been no injuries except for the passenger who became so excited that he turned a somersault out of a car window. A more serious accident took place on November 8, 1833. An axle on one car broke, derailing the train, which was running at twenty-five miles an hour, five miles above the usual limit because the crew was attempting to recover lost time. The resulting smashup was relatively serious. Ex-President John Quincy Adams was one of the passengers lucky enough to escape injury, but the steamboat king, Cornelius Vanderbilt, was not so fortunate. He suffered a crushed chest and afterwards (at least for a good many years) held firm to an oath that he would have nothing more to do with the steamcars.

The railroad as completed between South Amboy and Bordentown was working efficiently as a portage between Raritan Bay and the Delaware River. Steam-operated trains saved time, but an even better schedule would be possible once the railroad was built south, parallel to the Delaware River, to Camden. All effort was now concentrated on this portion of the line. It was finally opened in January of 1834, completing the projected sixty-one-mile railroad. The railroad was not really complete, however. Stevens and his partners were as nervous as ever that someone would invade their territory. They felt threatened from the north and south, despite the ironclad protection offered by the Marriage Act and its corollaries. The Philadelphia and Trenton was pushing its tracks ever northward, while the New Jersey Railroad and Transportation Company aimed toward its southern terminus at New Brunswick. Stockton was especially exercised about the P&T, which he felt was a menace to the canal's traffic.

Figure 55. The first passenger cars were built by
M. P. and M. E. Green of Hoboken, New Jersey,
in 1831. At first the cars were horse powered.
(*Harper's Weekly,* August 25, 1888.)

The Philadelphia and Trenton Railroad was a Pennsylvania corporation organized in 1832 to build a line between the Delaware River and Philadelphia. But it was looking beyond these limitations and threatened to encroach into the private domain of the Joint Companies. The railroad opened in 1835 and had already purchased control of the Trenton and Delaware Bridge Company and the Trenton and New Brunswick Turnpike Company. (The bridge had opened earlier, in 1806, for pedestrian and wagon traffic.) The railroad laid rails on the north lane of the bridge and moved cars by horsepower directly into Trenton. Now it was feared that, once inside New Jersey, the P&T would find a way to expand northward using the turnpike for a right-of-way. This could never be permitted and so Stockton began to buy up the railroad's stock. The C&A joined their old ally and issued $825,000 in silver bonds to complete the purchase.* By 1836 the P&T was part of the Joint Companies, although it maintained the fiction of being a separate corporation. In September of that year the P&T, acting as a puppet, agreed to help build a new railroad to New Brunswick, thus making a direct rail link between Philadelphia, Trenton, and New Brunswick. The NJRR & T, opened in 1836, would carry passengers on to Jersey City to a ferry connecting Manhattan with the New Jersey mainland. The new line would of course parallel the old C&A main line roughly seven miles to the south. A branch from Bordentown to Trenton linking the system together was opened in 1838.

---

* Never to be outdone, the Joint Companies were accused of making a neat profit by securing a corner on the stock and driving its price well above par, to $250 a share.

Figure 56. Passengers ended their steamboat ride from New York at these docks in South Amboy. The steamer is the *John Potter* or the *Joseph Belknap*. (*Gleason's Pictorial,* April 1, 1854.)

Figure 57. This remarkable photograph shows the C&A steamer terminal in Manhattan on the Hudson River in 1865. (Courtesy of the Frederick S. Lightfoot Collection.)

The panic of 1837 slowed financing of the new main line, but work was finally begun in June 1838. The track at the line's southern end paralleled the Delaware and Raritan Canal's serpentine path from Trenton via Princeton to a point just west of Kingston. It then raced northward on a relatively straight line to New Brunswick. Through-service was inaugurated on January 1, 1839. The south side of the old tollbridge at Trenton was remodeled and strengthened to carry locomotive-propelled trains, but because of differing track gauges, passengers were obliged to change cars at Trenton. This annoyance was removed the following year, when the P&T was regauged to the 4-foot 10-inch width of its parent.

Passengers could now go between New York and Philadelphia entirely by rail except for the ferry ride across the Hudson. Through cars were offered; however, each railroad provided its own locomotives and crew. The trip took 5½ hours, a saving of nearly 1½ hours over the South Amboy route. Needless to say, the traffic began to shift to the all-rail route. By 1860 almost three times as many passengers were going via the land route. But even before this superior service was offered, traffic was growing remarkably. It had in fact been good from the very first day.

Rival stage operators tried to frighten travelers away from rail travel. One resorted to the following statement in a newspaper advertisement, in which potential passengers were warned of "the great danger and inconvenience which they are subject to in traveling on crooked railroads, so often experienced in consequence of the cars getting off the tracks at the curves and turnouts, and thereby liable to upset." But the public was not dissuaded, despite such cautionary notices or the reports of actual accidents. In 1833,

even before the line was fully opened, some 109,900 persons were carried over the C&A. Within six years, the yearly total was approaching twice that figure, and during the busiest seasons 1,000 passengers a day were handled. By 1850 the yearly total approached 350,000, and by the time of Lincoln's first year in office it was around 480,000. Investment, profits, and the physical plant kept pace with this growth in traffic.

In 1840 the C&A had 17 locomotives, 71 passenger and baggage cars, 65 freight cars, and 8 steamboats. Its investment amounted to $3 million. Toward the end of its corporate life, the Camden and Amboy, as part of the United Companies, was a major element in a substantial transportation system that operated 128 locomotives, 233 passenger cars, 1,090 freight cars, 15 steamboats, and a small fleet of tugs, car floats, and schooners. One hundred trains a day—twelve offered through service between New York and Philadelphia—carried six million passengers a year. Investment in 1869 was $30.5 million.

The stockholders were far more interested in the bottom line than in any other statistic the scant annual reports of the Joint Companies might offer. Year after year they had every reason to be pleased. Monopoly was not without profit. Most early railroads were marginal moneymakers. Most were overwhelmed by huge fixed debts, scant operating capital, wildly fluctuating traffic levels, and competing lines. This was never true for the C&A. It was exceptional, almost blessed among America's pioneer corporations; it seemed immune to the common cares that plagued the American railroad industry in general. It never wanted for capital, traffic, or cash. It was protected from the undignified scramble for business by a devoted and protective state

Figure 58. Highway overpass at Bordentown in the 1840s. The watchman and bell are presumably ready to alert the passengers in the open shed at the track level that a train is approaching. (*Historical Collections of New Jersey,* 1844.)

government. Its enemies and critics were blankly ignored by its even more powerful friends. For forty years the Camden and Amboy moved regally about its royal preserve safe from all predators. And when it finally expired it was by its own decree and at its own price. Between 1830 and 1860, good times and bad, dividends were never less than 6 percent and ran as high as 30. In 1833, for example, gross receipts of $468,000 yielded a net profit of $181,000. In 1860 the gross was $1,907,000 and the net was $735,000. Nine years later, after its merger into the United Companies, the new firm reported a gross of $7.8 million and a profit of $2.9 million. These healthy earnings were a result of a large traffic and high fares, the latter being the focus for much public discussion. The through fare was normally four dollars, but the road charged an extra dollar on night trains during a few years. This made the fare nearly five cents a mile, nearly twice the national average. Protest over this matter reached a peak in the late 1840s. The state and even the federal government refused to take any action. At last the railroad became so concerned over the public outcry that the fare was quietly reduced to three dollars in September of 1849.

During the flurry of this debate in the press, the New Jersey state officials hoped the entire affair would soon blow over. They had a very cozy arrangement. The monopoly paid enough to satisfy the state debt, meet its own annual expenses, and very often leave a surplus. The state owned 1/15th of the C&A common stock and thus enjoyed a large and regular dividend payment. The transit duty by itself produced 20 percent of the state's income: between 1830 and 1848 the state received over $670,000 from this tax alone. There were of course persistent accusations that

Figure 59. A swing bridge on the C&A Railroad's Princeton branch. The scene is dated sometime in the 1860s. (Courtesy of Thomas T. Taber.)

other monies were paid directly to various civil servants. H. V. Poor in his *History of the Railroads and Canals of the United States* (1860) directly accused the Joint Companies of a studious concealment of their finances. Because their accounts were closed to public inspection, felonious payments were possible. In his *Congressional History of Railways,* Lewis H. Haney claimed that the monopoly maintained itself by wholesale corruption. Few state officials were ready to end the lucrative association with the Joint Companies. It was a monopoly? So what! The state had given special privileges to turnpikes and other groups in the past; what was wrong with helping this local enterprise so ably led by Stevens and Stockton? The state seemed ready to strengthen rather than dissolve the union. In addition to the Marriage Act, the state entered into an even more friendly agreement. In 1837 it was agreed that the surplus on any through fare over three dollars would be shared equally by the railroad and the state. Seventeen years later, new legislation added nine years to the corporation's life.

The United States Congress showed an equal reluctance to throttle the Joint Companies. In 1848 merchants of New York appealed for relief from the evil effects of monopoly. They spoke of high fares together with discriminatory treatment of New Jersey citizens who could travel as way passengers at reduced rates even when they traveled the entire line. They spoke about unconscionable delays to the U.S. mail because the Joint Companies refused to operate special trains to handle it more expeditiously. Congress debated. Some members felt it was a question for the courts, others simply wanted to table the matter, while the majority finally referred the matter to the Post Office Committee,

Figure 60. Bridge over the Raritan River at New Brunswick, New Jersey, in 1866. It was near here that the C&A and NJRR&T exchanged freight and passengers.

where it quietly died. During the traffic peak of the Civil War, when so many new travelers were exposed to the misery and inconvenience of traveling between New York and Washington over five separate railroads, the question of the Joint Companies came up again in the national chambers. Commodore Stockton declared that the federal government had no jurisdiction over a railroad that operated wholly within a single state. He cited the historic decision rendered in *Gibbons* v. *Ogden,* which limited Washington to regulation of interstate commerce. Not all members were convinced by this narrow interpretation of the law, and no less a member of Congress than Charles Sumner delivered a bitter address against the monopoly on February 14, 1865. Again the friends of the Joint Companies prevailed, but only after the northeastern railroads belatedly improved service between Manhattan and the nation's capital.

Service had actually improved over the years to a measurable degree, both in speed and frequency. The 1851 *American Railway Guide* listed fourteen trains a day on the South Amboy line. Four of these were through trains; the remainder were locals. The first steamer left New York at 8:00 A.M. and the last boat departed at 4:00 in the afternoon. The boat trip took one-and-a-half hours. The total trip over this route, including a fifteen-minute ferry ride across the Delaware, took between four hours and fifteen minutes and four hours and twenty-five minutes. More frequent service was offered over the land route via Trenton. Thirty-five trains ran a day; six of them offered through service. The fastest train made the trip in four hours and ten minutes, proving to be only a small saving over the water route. Six years later, *Lloyd's American Guide* noted a decline in speed of service over the South Amboy route. The fastest

service now consumed five hours and five minutes, and one journey took nine hours and thirty-five minutes. The superiority of the land route was no doubt so obvious that the managers were apparently disinclined to push for fast schedules on the South Amboy line, and it was allowed to fall away to local service. In June 1869 the *Official Guide* listed one hundred trains a day on the United Companies lines; a dozen through trains a day were running between New York and Philadelphia. The fastest schedule was three hours and thirty minutes. Slower through trains, listed as accommodations, took as long as four hours and forty minutes.

The Camden and Amboy could boast only of a middling safety record. In fact the less said about it the better. It was certainly nothing like the NJRR&T, which was almost a model in this account. For most of its history the New Jersey line never killed a revenue passenger. But the C&A began to maim and exterminate its patrons from the beginning of steam operations. There were no major disasters, however, until August 29, 1855. The up, or northbound, late-morning train arrived in Burlington as scheduled. It waited and then proceeded on the single-track line. The opposing train was then sighted and the eight-car up train was obliged to stop and back into a passing siding three miles to the south. It proceeded to do so at about fifteen miles an hour. Down the line a local doctor was approaching the track. He knew the schedule and was sure the line was temporarily clear of trains. He noticed the backing train just short of the crossing and drew his team to a stop, but his horses bolted and dashed in front of the rear car and derailed it. The engineer did not notice the accident at first, and the train continued to move until the rear car, af-

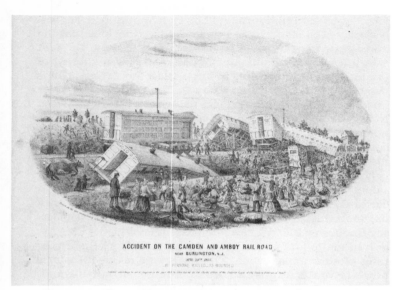

Figure 61. The accident near Burlington, New Jersey, in August 1855. The number of casualties listed in the caption fails to include two victims. (Smithsonian Neg. 5058.)

ter bouncing across the ties, rolled over into the ditch and in so doing pulled the second rear car across the track. The following car crashed into it. The splintering coaches killed twenty-three passengers and injured many more (fig. 61). Curiously, the doctor and his two passengers escaped with only injuries.

The accident caused a public furor that was easily excited against a corporation already held in low esteem because of high fares and allegations of political and financial malfeasance. Just two years before, a head-on collision claimed four lives. And in another incident, in April 1853, part of a train dropped through an open drawbridge into Rancocas Creek (fig. 62). No passenger cars fell into the drink but a majority of travelers, no doubt, felt like one at the end of this particular journey. Other lines had more catastrophic wrecks, but the C&A had enough mishaps to aggravate and frighten the traveling public. Yet the line, despite its huge traffic and profits, refused to take any substantial measures, such as double tracking, until the 1860s. Another accident in 1865, on the P&T, which killed six and wounded forty, prompted Ashbel Welch (1809–1882), vice president and engineer of the C&A, to install telegraphic-manual block signaling on the railroad that would stop the train unless it was specifically notified that the track was clear of other trains. Welch's signals were installed all the way to Jersey City within two years. Welch continued to lobby for greater safety even after the PRR lease. He recommended installation of one of the first interlocking plants in North America to control the busy junction at East Newark. And in 1870 Welch ordered installation of a small interlocking machine near Trenton.

Despite these late efforts at reform, the railroad was actu-

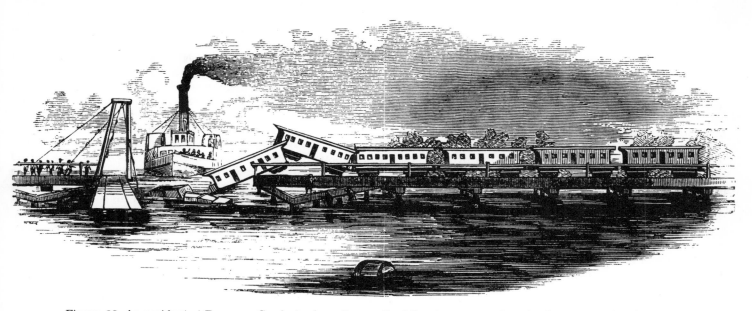

Figure 62. An accident at Rancocas Creek, twelve miles north of Camden, occurred on April 23, 1853. A swing bridge was opened for the steamer, but no one signaled the train. (*London Illustrated News,* May 7, 1853.)

ally run in a parsimonious fashion for most of its history. The original line was built on a better plan than most early United States lines, but there was no major effort at upgrading the property. The C&A continued to operate as a single-track railroad despite a continuous rise in traffic. The connecting NJRR&T double-tracked its main line between 1855 and 1859 and installed heavy rail to ensure safety and avoid delays. Not so the C&A. It was too stingy. Nor would it upgrade the twisting tracks that followed the canal between Trenton and Kingston. Passengers who were jostled from side to side in their seats as the train snaked its way through an endless series of curves had daily cause to curse the monopoly. This portion of the line was finally abandoned in 1864 as part of a general improvement program undertaken by the several railroads connecting New York and Washington. A new double track, on a vastly improved alignment with only four curves, was constructed in its place. Princeton was bypassed in the process and to placate its residents a branch was opened that has since carried thousands of students between the campus and Princeton Junction.

Not long after double tracking was finished, the Joint Companies began negotiations with their neighbor to the north. For years they had had a working relationship with the NJRR&T, but it could hardly have been called a friendly arrangement. The Joint Companies' interest in absorbing their northern connection was always evident, and officers of the New Jersey line could never trust so powerful and avaricious a neighbor. Memories of the P&T takeover were still fresh. However, the old officers of the NJRR&T had either died or retired by the mid-1860s, and the new officers were less militant about a merger. Perhaps they saw it

as inevitable. The Joint Companies had already secured a charter for a new line that would bypass the existing exchange of cars and establish a single line between Philadelphia and New York, controlled entirely by the monopoly. Pragmatism finally overcame sentiment and pride: the NJRR&T joined the monopoly in January 1867 as a partner in the United Companies of New Jersey. Technically all of the partners remained separate legal corporations and shared revenues and expenses mutually, but the new board of directors was dominated by the Camden and Amboy members. Poor's *Manual of Railroads* for 1870–71 summarized the firm's physical plant in an outline (*right*).

The United Companies was soon to be courted by ambitious trunklines in the area. The Reading was eager to find a route into the New York Harbor area—a marriage was proposed. The Pennsylvania Railroad correctly saw the United lines as part of its master plan to reach New York and work its way south, where its president, Thomas A. Scott, was trying to assemble a rail network. The Pennsylvania had greater resources than the Reading could hope to muster and so talks, which began early in 1869, grew ever more serious with the Philadelphia-based giant. A 999-year lease was announced effective July 1, 1871, in which the lessor agreed to guarantee a 10 percent dividend on United's capital of $19.4 million. It would also guarantee to pay its bonded debt of some $17 million. The United Companies, in addition to the properties listed earlier in this discussion, had so-called liquid assets amounting to $4 million-worth of cash, stocks, and bonds. Some stockholders opposed the lease and secured a court injunction that delayed the lease until December 1, 1871. After that time the rail lines of the United Companies became the New

1. *Owned directly by the Companies:*

Philadelphia (Kensington), Pa., to Trenton, N.J., all double track .... 26.6 miles.
Trenton, N.J., to Jersey City, N.J., all double track .... 57.1 "
Camden, N.J., to South Amboy, N.J., 20 miles double track .... 61.2 "
Bordentown, N.J., to Trenton, N.J. .... 6.1 "
Jamesburg, N.J., to Monmouth Junction, N.J. .... 5.5 "
Monmouth Junction, N.J., to Kingston, N.J. .... 4.0 "
Princeton Branch, 3 miles; other branches, 1.5 .... 4.5 "

     Total owned directly .... 165.0 miles.

2. *Railroads in which the Companies have a controlling interest:*

Rocky Hill to Kingston .... 2.5 miles.   Cape May to Millville .... 41.0 miles.
Burlington to Mount Holly .... 7.1 "   Salem Branch .... 17.0 "
Mount Holly to near Camden .... 16.5 "   Freehold to Jamesburg .... 11.5 "
Pemberton to Mount Holly .... 5.9 "   Millstone to New Brunswick .... 6.6 "
Vincentown Branch .... 3.0 "   Perth Amboy to Woodbridge .... 6.4 "
Glassboro to Bridgton .... 37.0 "   Belvidere-Delaware RR .... 68.7 "
Millville to Glassboro .... 32.0 "   Flemington Branch RR .... 11.4 "

     Total in which the Companies have a controlling interest .... 259.6 miles.

3. *Other leased railroads:*

Connecting Railroad, 6.8 miles; Pemberton and Hightstown Railroad, 24.5 miles .... 31.3 "
     Total railroad line owned, leased and controlled .... 445.9 miles.

The "Delaware and Raritan Canal," forming an important part of the United Companies' properties, is described thus:

Bordentown (Delaware River), N.J., to New Brunswick (Raritan River), N.J. .... 43.0 miles.
Bull's Island (Delaware River), N.J., to Trenton, N.J. .... 22.5 "

     Total .... 65.0 miles.

Thus the United Companies own, operate or control 65 miles of canal and 456 miles of railroad, and, including double track 106 miles, and sidings, etc., 74 miles, in all 636 miles of track.

Rolling Stock.—Locomotive engines, 128. Cars—passenger, 193; baggage and mail, 40; house and stock, 612; platform, mail and line, 478—total, 1,323 cars. In addition to this list, each auxiliary railroad has a full equipment of its own.

Floating Stock.—Steamboats—passenger, 3; ferry, 12; freight, 4; towing, 14—total steamboats, 33; freight barges, 5; car floats, carrying 8 to 10 freight cars each, 10; schooners, 20; coal barges, 21; canal boats, 77.

Figure 63. Advertisement for through service between New York and Washington, D.C., appeared in the *Official Guide,* June 1870.

York Division of the Pennsylvania Railroad.

Over the next few years the leased lines gradually lost their identity and were reshaped as an indistinguishable part of the Standard Railroad of the World. The headquarters was moved to Jersey City. The Bordentown shops were closed. The locomotives were renumbered in 600 and 700 series, but as soon as possible, standard PRR engines took their place. The tracks were regauged to Pennsy's compromise of 4 feet 9 inches, and right-hand operations were adopted.

The railroad itself was gradually remodeled so that in time much of the original roadbed simply disappeared. The ancient wooden bridge over the Delaware was replaced with an iron structure in 1875. It, in turn, was replaced by steel in 1898. In 1903 a great stone viaduct was built downstream. At about the same time the railroad was realigned, and major parts of it were elevated to avoid street crossings in the densely settled communities that now lined the tracks. Automatic signaling and four tracks boosted the capacity, speed, and safety of the railroad beyond the most optimistic dreams of any pioneer railroad man, save perhaps Robert L. Stevens, who envisioned a grand steel highway at least approaching the new superrailroad that cut across eastern New Jersey. As a final step the snorting steam locomotive was banished in favor of nearly silent electric traction. The wires did not come all at once, however. The line started with a short electric segment to service New York's Penn Station in 1910. A few years later suburban lines around Philadelphia were converted, and finally in 1928 plans were announced for electric service between New York and Washington. In 1933 such trains began to operate between Philadelphia and New York. Two years later the project was completed. Schedules varied from train to train and from year to year, but in general the entire run of 225 miles can be easily made in four hours with conventional equipment. Efforts to improve this schedule began in earnest in the 1960s. There was talk about 160-mph trains, but the Metroliners, introduced in 1969, have never even approached such speeds in regular service. For a short time 120-mph schedules were attempted, but for reasons of safety, comfort, and cost they were abandoned for a more relaxed pace. At the present time $2.5 billion is being pumped into rebuilding the entire Northeast Corridor line between Washington and Boston. A completion date remains uncertain, but it is hoped that in not too many years from the time of this writing, high-speed electric trains will be running on the corridor. The new trains that are projected to rocket across New Jersey at more than two miles a minute will follow in part the path once traversed in such a deliberate and smoky fashion by the creations of Isaac Dripps and Robert L. Stevens so many years ago.

A Note on Sources

Because so much has already been written on the corporate history of the C&A, I have not attempted to produce an original research paper but rather have summarized the work of others that is available in most major libraries. For that reason I have deleted footnotes in this chapter in favor of a listing of my sources as outlined in the bibliography.

Bibliography

Barton, Roger A. "The Camden and Amboy Railroad Monopoly." *Proceedings of the New Jersey Historical Society,* Oct. 1927, pp. 405–18.

Burgess, George H., and Miles C. Kennedy.*Centennial History of the Pennsylvania Railroad Company* Philadelphia, 1949.

Flint, Henry M. *Railroads of the United States: Their History and Statistics.* Philadelphia, 1868.

Freeman, Leslie E., Jr. "The New Jersey Railroad and Transportation Company." Railway and Locomotive Historical Society, Bulletin 88 (May 1953), pp. 100–59.

Haney, Lewis H. *A Congressional History of Railways.* Madison, Wis., 1908.

Lane, Wheaton J. *From Indian Trail to Iron Horse: Travel and Transportation in New Jersey from 1620 to 1860.* Princeton, 1939.

Meyer, B. H. *The History of Transportation in the United States Before 1860.* Washington, D.C., 1917.

Poor, Henry V. *History of the Railroads and Canals of the United States of America.* New York, 1860.

_____. *Manual of the Railroads of the United States.* 1st ed. New York, 1868.

Shaw, Robert B. *A History of Railroad Accidents.* 1978 (pub. by the author).

Stow, F. H. *The Capitalist's Guide and Railway Manual.* New York, 1859.

Tanner, H. S. *Railroads of the United States.* New York, 1840.

Turnbull, A. D. *John Stevens: An American Record.* New York, 1928.

Warren, J. G. H. *A Century of Locomotive Building by Robert Stephenson & Co., 1823–1923.* Newcastle, England, 1923.

Watkins, J. E. *Ceremonies Upon the Completion of the Monument Erected by the Pennsylvania Railroad at Bordentown, New Jersey.* Washington, D.C., 1891.

White, John H., Jr. *American Locomotives, 1830–1880: An Engineering History.* Baltimore, 1968.

Wilson, William B. *History of the Pennsylvania Railroad Co.* 2 vols. Philadelphia, 1895.

Appendix A: Testing the John Bull, 1980

William L. Withuhn

The Smithsonian's decision in 1980 to steam and run the *John Bull* was not a "decision" in the ordinary sense, but an evolution. Each step of the rehabilitation carried with it the real possibility that, because of what was learned at that step, the project would be dropped as not feasible. The paramount consideration was the risk of damage to the locomotive. The *John Bull* is a unique historical artifact, important both to the nation's technological history and to the history of the Smithsonian collections. Its continued preservation in uncompromised condition was and is the primary objective: steaming and operation had to take place with that objective constantly in view.

In January 1980, John White authorized an initial test of the locomotive's rotating machinery, using compressed air. A museum crew under technician John N. Stine began the preparation of the locomotive at its site on the first floor of the National Museum of American History.

The first step was a check to make sure the cylinders were in good shape and to see if the pistons, rods, and rear driving wheels would move freely. The museum crew removed the cylinder heads and found the cylinders clean and free of rust. Then the rear-axle journals, rod bearings, crossheads, and piston-rod packings were oiled. Some light oil was introduced from the steampipes into the cylinders so as to lubricate the pistons and valves. Access for oil into each outside steampipe was gained through a small threaded hole, preexisting in each pipe, which was then resealed with a pipe plug. Then with the front wheels tied down by cables to the rails, Stine and his crew jacked the rear wheels under the journal boxes, using wooden blocking to pad the boxes. The jacks raised the rear wheels about an inch off the rails, allowing the wheels to be turned by

Figure 64. Compressed air test, January 1980. John Stine is crouching on the front end of the frame. John White (right) and Larry Jones (left) stand on the rear deck. (Smithsonian Neg. 80-429-14.)

manual use of a crowbar against the spokes. All the machinery moved easily through a full revolution.

Next, the museum crew removed the old crosshead feedwater pumps, since White and Stine felt that these would not give a fully reliable source of feedwater in operation. (Injectors would be used instead.) The check valves were left on. The whistle was removed and, in its place, an adaptor was inserted for a high-pressure air line. A new gasket was made for the smokebox door, the cylinder heads were reinstalled with new gaskets, and all keys and nuts in the running gear were tightened. An adaptor was then made for the fitting of a small pressure gauge, using an existing threaded hole at the top of the Bury dome.

With the rear wheels jacked up, the front wheels secured to the rails, and air pressure supplied to the boiler, the front safety valve opened with a bang at 42 psi. John White pulled on the throttle. A cloud of dust erupted from the smokestack, and the rear wheels began turning—smoothly and quietly. The test on air pressure confirmed that the locomotive's power train was in substantially good order, pending further testing.

The following step was an extensive examination and test of the boiler. The wooden jacketing, of tongue-and-groove boards, was removed from the boiler barrel and steamdome; each piece was numbered and marked as to its location. The jacketing was found to be soft pine rather than oak; it may have been replaced by the Pennsylvania Railroad shops during the 1927 repairs. The removal of the jacketing uncovered a surprise: a permanently riveted coverplate was found over a large hole in the boiler shell under the present location of the bell. This hole corresponds to the specified location of the original manhole, before the dome was

Figure 65. Hartford Steam Boiler Inspection and Insurance Company's ultrasonic shear-wave unit was read by William Withuhn while testing for cracks. (Smithsonian Neg. 80-1-0798-14A.)

moved by Isaac Dripps. It seems unlikely that a duplicate boiler would include this now-purposeless hole. The riveting throughout the boiler is consistent with an 1831 construction date, except for the bottom half of the first barrel course, which appears to have been replaced at a relatively late date, perhaps in 1927. Thus the *John Bull*'s boiler appears to be the original.

The Hartford Steam Boiler Inspection and Insurance Company was engaged to perform the boiler inspection. Under supervising inspector David C. Spinelli, a Hartford crew conducted ultrasonic, magnaflux, and radiographic tests of the boiler and some of the running-gear parts from March 11 to 13, 1980.[1] Prior to these dates, Stine's crew, including machinist Larry Jones and assistant Jim Knowles, removed the lead truck and associated hardware, the cylinder heads, the smokebox door, the steamdome, the outside steampipes and throttle, the grates, the ashpan, the cleaninghole cover on the backhead, and two inspection plates at the mud ring. The tubes were cleaned out with a round wire brush on a long handle.

After an extensive visual inspection by Mr. Spinelli, Hartford technician Gerald Coursen and two assistants performed the other parts of their firm's on-site examination. Ultrasonic tests were used to determine wall thicknesses of boiler and firebox plates, as well as tube thicknesses. Magnafluxing was done to find cracks in cylinder walls, piston heads, rods, boiler rivets, and boiler seams. Radiographic tests (X-ray tests, in effect, using a small radioisotope source to expose filmplates taped over areas of interest on the boiler) were used to look for cracks in boiler welts and seams and to examine the internal quality of the boiler iron. Ultrasonic shear-wave tests were used to look for defects in cylinder walls and rods. Samples were taken of mud-leg scale and deposits, of boiler scale from the steam side of the front tubesheet, and of fireside deposits from the firebox crownsheet and from inside the tubes. These samples were sent to Hartford's chemical analytical laboratory.

During the course of taking down the right main rod, Stine discovered the top corner of the front end of the right main rod broken off, inside the area covered by the front rod strap. Stine and machinist Jones brazed the broken piece back on and ground it back to contour.

The Smithsonian crew then prepared the engine for a hydrostatic test. Such a test involves filling the boiler with water and then pressurizing the boiler with a small handpump up to (and above) the proposed operating pressure, in this case 50 psi. A pipe connection and globe valve were threaded into the existing hole on top of the steamdome normally occupied by the front safety valve; this connection allowed filling of the boiler with water. At the mud ring, the right blowdown cock was removed and a "tee" installed to allow connection of a pressurizing hose and a water-pressure gauge. The pressurizing hose was connected, in turn, to a handpump that supplied water from a 55-gallon drum that acted as a reservoir. Since the "hydro" test was performed at the *John Bull*'s normal site on the museum floor, precautions had to be taken against water spillage. A water vacuum was used to dry spills quickly, and hoses carried most runoff down to drains in the museum basement.

Before the first hydro test on March 26th, the steamdome, throttle, and boiler-inspection hole covers were reinstalled with new gaskets. The outside steampipes were left off, and the steam outlet connections on either side of the throttle were sealed with dummyplates and gaskets. As soon as any appreciable water pressure was applied in the first test, numerous leaks appeared: at both check valves (from the connecting flanges and from the check valves themselves), at the throttle gland, and at the whistle connection atop the steamdome. These items had to be plugged, repaired, or replaced.

The check valves were easily disconnected. The removal and resealing of the check-valve flanges on the boiler, however, turned out to be a major problem. The flanges are curved in order to conform to the shape of the boiler barrel, and the original bolts holding on the flanges were installed from inside the barrel, with the bolt heads inward. Each bolt has a unique alignment, due to the flanges' curvature; hence the flanges cannot be removed with the bolts in place, even with the outer nuts off. Stine devised a way to remove the flange bolts without losing them inside the boiler. For the bolts at the top of each flange, Stine tied strings to the outer ends of the bolts and pushed the bolts into the boiler. Each bolt was gently lowered to a point opposite the large center hole of the flange (where the check valve normally is fitted) and fished out of this hole. Fishing out the bolts was complicated by the presence inside the boiler of all the tubes and longitudinal stays, which necessitated a great deal of prying and bending to recover each bolt. With several of the bolts removed in this way, the flange could finally be pulled off and the remaining bolts withdrawn.

So that new check valves could be temporarily installed for use with injectors, new check-valve flangeplates were made of 5/16" boilerplate. The proper contour was determined with a pattern gauge and transferred to a piece of Masonite. The new plates were cut out and rolled to contour by the J. E. Hurley Company in Washington. Stine and Jones then drilled and installed the new plates, using the existing bolt holes in the boiler shell, with double-ended studs having nuts at each end. These studs were specially made so that the studs and their inner nuts could be loosely fitted to the boiler, the flanges fitted on over the outer ends of the studs, and the studs drawn up tight before the outer nuts were put on and tightened. This extra care was necessary to insure a leak-free installation.

On the second attempt at a hydro test on April 10, the throttle gland still leaked excessively, but the boiler was able to hold 40 psi with makeup pressure from the handpump every three or four seconds. Spinelli was able to make an inventory of small drips and leaks from various places on the inner and outer firebox sheets; all leaks appeared minor.

Stine removed the throttle entirely the following day and sealed the hole in the back of the steamdome with a dummyplate and gasket. On a third hydro test, the boiler could hold 50 psi on house water pressure through a garden hose, without aid of the handpump. Meanwhile, the throttle was lapped in by the Jensen Manufacturing Company of Alexandria, Virginia, and the gland repacked with Teflon packing by Stine.

While these operations were going on, White asked me to calculate the horsepower and tractive effort of the *John Bull* at a working pressure of 40 psi. The standard formulae gave a tractive effort at starting of 1,434 lbs. and a drawbar pull at starting (tractive effort less resistance) of 934 lbs. Standard allowances for the resistance of curves, grades, and speeds indicated that the *John Bull* could handle the Camden and Amboy coach No. 3 with a full load of

Figure 66. David Spinelli, inspector for the Hartford Company, works a pump during one of the hydrostatic tests. (Smithsonian Neg. 80-10802-12.)

passengers up a 1 percent grade at 5 mph, and with a few degrees of curve included. The little locomotive would be able to handle the moderate stretches of the Georgetown branch.[2]

An interesting point was learned in performing the tractive-effort calculation. Assuming that half the weight of the engine is carried on the rearmost axle (the driven axle), the factor of adhesion works out to be 6.96 to 1, or nearly seven pounds of weight on drivers for every pound of tractive effort. Such a high adhesion factor indicates that the full tractive force of the engine at 40 psi can be developed at the single pair of drivers without slipping. Even if the boiler pressure were raised to 70 psi, which may have been the original setting, and the tractive effort increased thereby, the factor of adhesion with one driving axle would be nearly 4:1, still high enough to permit good traction. Hence, when the Camden and Amboy disconnected the front pair of drivers in the 1830s in order to fit the lead truck, the pulling power of the locomotive was not compromised. The locomotive's pulling force was determined by her boiler pressure and cylinder dimensions, and all her available power could be put to use without adhesion loss by a single driving axle. Stevens and Dripps may have suspected this fact before the *John Bull*'s modification, and they probably confirmed it in practice afterward. In fact, disconnecting the forward driving axle cut the machine resistance and thus may have increased the drawbar pull at all speeds, although marginally at best.

John Stine then asked me for advice on the proper size of the injectors. To this end, a calculated evaporation was worked out.[3] The previous arithmetic showed a maximum potential cylinder horsepower of 38 at speed. The maximum expected evaporation worked out to be 1,650 to 2,400 lbs. of steam per hour. Two Penberthy injectors, model AA528, were judged adequate, with each of them able to handle an average evaporation of 1,000 lbs. per hour.

The throttle was refitted to the steamdome, and two small, manually operated lubricators were made and fitted into the existing threaded holes at the front ends of the outside steampipes. (Each homemade lubricator consisted of a small piece of pipe to act as an oil reservoir, a filling plug at the top, and a small piece of connecting pipe with petcock at the bottom. These lubricators provided oil for valves and cylinders.)

At the steamdome, the old spring safety valve was removed and a one-inch-thick plate was cut, drilled, and tapped for a large Kunkle 50-psi toggle safety valve; the mountingplate and gasket fit the existing holes at the top of the dome. An adaptor was made for the whistle mounting hole, so that the "original" *John Bull* whistle could be installed.

The old spring-balance safety valve behind the bell was removed and a dummyplate installed to seal the opening. A smaller Kunkle 50-psi toggle safety valve was installed by means of a "tee" into an existing hole at the top of the Bury dome on the left side. The tee also provided mounting for a 60-psi Trerice steam-pressure gauge; the new gauge provided backup for the large steam pressure gauge mounted on top of the Bury dome. It was last calibrated in 1927.

A sight glass for checking the water level was added by removing the top and bottom tricocks and installing a short Conbraco water glass, with valves and draincock, in the resulting holes. Jones threaded the sight-glass mounts to fit the existing original threads in the outer firebox sheet; the middle tricock was removed and its hole plugged.

When the injectors were received, these were plumbed into a new feedwater system for the locomotive. Existing lines that had served as steam-heating lines to the water-delivery pipes were removed. Removal of the heating lines opened a hole at the top center of the Bury dome, into which another "tee" was fitted. The tee was connected by unions to a pair of globe valves, one on either side of the Bury, which then served as the injector control valves, each regulating the flow of boiler steam to one of the injectors mounted under the footboard. Delivery lines from the injectors were run forward to the new check valves on the boiler. Each check valve fed into the boiler through a globe valve; the latter served as an isolation valve in case a check valve stuck open.

Water supply to the injectors came from the tender, which had to be replumbed. The *John Bull*'s tender has for many years been stored at the Smithsonian's Silver Hill, Maryland, facility, and the tender work was done there. The old iron cistern leaked, so it was removed. Two 250-gallon tanks (new fuel-oil tanks) were substituted and set on end on the tender floor. Valves were mounted into the sides of the tanks near the floor and these valves connected to water lines running below. In order to provide flexible connections between the tender's under-floor water lines and the injectors mounted on the engine below the footboard, standard railroad air hoses and gladhands were used to carry the water from tender to locomotive. Isolation valves were installed on either side of each hose connection, to stem any unexpected leaks that might develop. Filling of each water tank was provided by an opening cut into the top of the tank; a wooden cover served to close the fill opening when not in use and also allowed visual inspection of the water level in the tank. (After the October 14 test run on the Warrenton branch, a new open replica tender was made in the museum workshop.)

All the modifications, to tender and locomotive alike, were regarded as strictly temporary for the purpose of the 1980–81 anniversary runs. No structural changes of any kind were made; no new holes of any sort were made into the boiler. After consideration of the boiler examination results, no repairs were judged necessary to the boiler prior to the October 14th steaming. And all parts temporarily removed were carefully catalogued for eventual replacement on the locomotive. The first priority, that of preservation of the machine, was met.

When the rehabilitation work was complete, John White arranged for a trial run of the engine under steam. With superb cooperation from the Southern Railway, the test took place on that company's Warrenton branch (Calverton to Warrenton) in northern Virginia, on October 13–14, 1980.

The test was a revelation. A metaphor from John Steinbeck most eloquently expresses the effects of that run both on our understanding of the *John Bull* and on ourselves as historians:

The Mexican sierra [a fish] has "XVII-15-IX" spines in the dorsal fin. These can easily be counted. But if the sierra strikes hard on the line so that our hands are burned, if the fish sounds and nearly escapes and finally comes in over the rail, his colors pulsing and his tail beating the air, a whole new relational externality has come into being—an entity which is more than the sum of the fish plus the fisherman. The only way to count the spines of the sierra unaffected by this second relational reality is to sit in a laboratory, open an evil-smelling jar, remove a still colorless fish from formalin solution, count the spines, and write the truth "D. XVII-15-IX." There you have recorded a reality which cannot be assailed—probably the least important reality concerning either the fish or yourself.[4]

Thus in 1980, the little *John Bull,* specimen of the Industrial Revolution, came out of its figurative bottle of formalin and regained life for a time. In the course of firing up and operating the engine, we gained several fresh and important insights into the history and design of the locomotive. These insights could only have come from the actual, hands-on experience of running and operating the engine.

The free steaming and easy draft of the locomotive were surprises for most of us. As soon as the first fire was lit on the 13th, a natural, soft draft began pulling the smoke up the stack, without any artificial aid by way of blower or other device. When the engine was under way, the ample furnace volume and relatively large steam room provided by the Bury firebox made for a very forgiving engine in terms of firing; there was no difficulty in bringing the steam back to pressure after neglecting the fire, and the engine operated well at almost any pressure between 25 and 50 psi. (We generally kept the pressure over 30 psi, to insure smooth operation of the injectors.)

Throttle and valve gear operated easily. The old "drophook" valve gear took some getting used to, as there is no provision for changing cutoff. The gear is engaged in forward, reverse, or neutral position. To shift from one position to the other, the operator has to disengage the valve links from their valves, manually realign the valves using

Figure 67. The engine and tender en route to Calverton, Virginia, on October 13, 1980, for an operating test under steam. (Courtesy of William L. Withuhn.)

the two long operating levers mounted on the backhead, and drop (or pull) the hooked links into the new position. One must perform this operation independently for each side of the engine, and the throttle must be shut off. On the October 14th run, we generally found it easiest to change valve-gear position with the engine stopped and with two people to help out: whoever was running the engine operated the link handles and valve levers at the rear footboard, while the second person observed the valve linkage at the front of the engine and told the operator when the correct engagement had been found. After a time, however, we began to get a proper "feel" for the valve-gear machinery. One person, unaided, could change the gear fairly quickly from the footboard, even while the train was still rolling when approaching a stop. The original operators of the *John Bull*, therefore, must have developed similar skills, permitting the valve gear to be disengaged and reengaged smoothly for quick changes of direction. The valve gear turned out to be much less ungainly and easier to operate than it had always appeared.

There was a major revelation in the mechanical design area. The locomotive rode and tracked with remarkable smoothness. At all speeds, the little engine had no yaw whatsoever, and she tracked with uncanny smoothness through curves and over occasional sections of poorly aligned rail. The lead truck seemed to be the secret.

In discussions of the *John Bull* written after the 1880s, the most that is usually said about the lead truck is that it served as the mounting point for "the first locomotive cowcatcher," and little credit is given to whatever guiding properties the truck may have had, beyond being a crude improvement over the lack of guidance in the original 0-4-0

Figure 68. October 14, 1980: the engine's first movement under its own power in fifty-three years—Calverton, Virginia, at the Southern Railway's Warrenton branch. (Smithsonian Neg. 80-17185-7A.)

configuration. The mechanical properties of the *John Bull*'s lead truck have been underrated, judging from our experience in 1980.

If the geometry of the truck is carefully examined, a strong case can be made that the *John Bull* is a 4-2-0. The yoke of the lead truck serves as the laterally rigid side frames of a four-wheel truck, locking the transverse centerlines of the lead-truck axle and the first big, nondriven axle into a parallel configuration. The yoke is cross-braced against distortion in the transverse plane, and the first two axles must track together in parallel, as a single truck. The essential feature is that the yoke is connected to the outer ends of the first big axle, not merely to the locomotive frame. Hence, the lead axle steers the first large axle; fore-and-aft free play is explicitly provided for in the pedestal jaws for the axle boxes of the large axle.

If the lead axle forms a four-wheel truck with the first large axle, how is this "truck" geometrically suspended in relation to the rest of the locomotive? The truck suspension forms a classic tripod, with one point of suspension being the front yoke spring and the other two points being the springs for the large idle axle. (If the front yoke spring is not connected, the steering properties are unchanged, but the lead axle carries less weight.) The "four-wheel lead truck" is well suspended for its guiding function, with all three springs bearing the load of the front of the locomotive and the truck permitted to swivel relative to the main frame of the engine.

The truck rigging definitely improves the running stability of the locomotive. The fast schedules kept by the Camden and Amboy engines, like the *John Bull,* no longer seem quite so surprising after our experience on the Calverton-

Figure 70. The *John Bull* shrouded in a cloud of steam escaping from the forward safety valve. (Courtesy of Robert M. Vogel.)

Figure 69. Trailing a light plume of wood smoke, the *John Bull* moves across the Virginia countryside in a display of railroading in its first decade. (Courtesy of Herbert H. Harwood, Jr.)

Figure 71. The crew poses with the engine at midday. Left to right: Larry Jones, John White, John Stine, and William Withuhn. (Courtesy of Robert M. Vogel.)

Casanova run. How the *John Bull*'s rigging may have affected subsequent lead-truck design is problematic; the much more elegant and influential four-wheel truck of John B. Jervis appeared on the *Brother Jonathan* of the Mohawk and Hudson Railroad in 1832, before the *John Bull* was modified.[5] (Perhaps the *John Bull* modification was an attempt to get four-wheel lead-truck guiding properties, in light of the spreading reputation of Jervis.) At any rate, the *John Bull*'s truck anticipates the two-wheel Hudson-type lead truck of 1864 in one important regard: the lead axle is suspended with (and partially equalized with) the first large axle in the main frame of the locomotive. In the *John Bull*'s truck, the front yoke spring acts as a fulcrum between the lead axle and first large axle, resulting in a partial equalization. Such equalization may not have been intended or fully appreciated by Stevens or Dripps, but the effect was to improve still further the riding qualities of the entire suspension.

Another major discovery made in running the *John Bull* was the "differential axle," with one wheel loose, found incorporated into the first large wheel pair. Nowhere in any record or extant publication is there mention of this unique axle design, which apparently was intended to allow each wheel on the nondriven large axle to turn at a different rate when the locomotive rounded a curve. Why such an axle arrangement was thought necessary on a railroad blessed with large-radius curves is not obvious, but the axle is undoubtedly the work of either Dripps or Stevens, who, again, did not seem content with orthodox solutions to mechanical problems.

The "loose wheel" was discovered during the unloading of the *John Bull* from its highway trailer at Calverton. As the

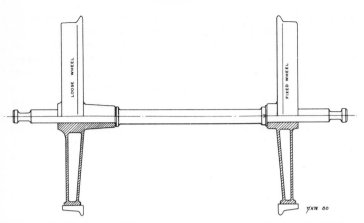

LOOSE WHEEL

FIXED WHEEL

J.H.W. 80

Figure 72. Diagram of the loose axle-and-wheel arrangement of the front pair of large wheels.

engine was being winched down on blocking to the rails, John White noticed one wheel on the first large axle turn slightly, while the other wheel on the axle did not. At first it looked as if we had a broken axle or some other equally disastrous difficulty. After the engine was down on the track, we used a tieplate as a "skate" under one wheel, while we moved the locomotive forward. As White had discovered, one wheel was indeed loose. We thought a key might be missing in the fit between hub and axle, but as confirmed later by John Stine, the loose wheel was clearly intentional and built with an extra-large hub to allow the axle and wheel to move differentially. On straight track, the loose wheel and axle would rotate at the same rate and so the wheel would act as a normal, fixed wheel. Even on curves, the differential movement was so slight that lubrication was probably unnecessary when the locomotive was in everyday service. The number of other early Camden and Amboy engines that may have had this design feature is unknown; perhaps Stevens or Dripps regarded it as an experiment that later proved unneeded. As demonstrated later in the evolution of railroad vehicle design, the taper in the tread of rail wheels allows such wheels to negotiate curves without excessive tread wear or axle stress, even though the axles are solid.

When the loose wheel and axle were applied to the *John Bull* is not clear. Anyone who has examined the engine carefully has noticed that the wheels on the first large axle do not match. One wheel has flat rather than curved felloes and no separate tire. It appears in the earliest known photograph of the locomotive (fig. 17), and yet it is the fixed wheel. The loose wheel, having the extra-long interior hub, matches the two rear driving wheels in overall design and

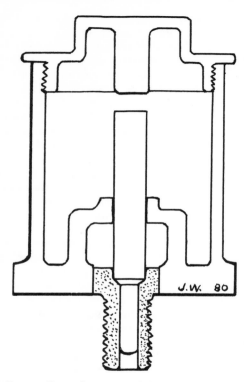

Figure 73. Brass oil cup from one of the main connecting rods. It probably dates from the 1876 restoration.

shape.

Another discovery made by White during the test was the ingenious style of oil cup on the back end of each main rod. Superficially each cup looked like an ordinary gravity brass cup: a simple reservoir that allowed oil to lubricate the bearing through a small hole. However, there is a plunger or piston in the hole that lifts open when the rod is on the upswing and falls closed by its own weight when the engine is at rest. In this way oil is conserved and reaches the bearing surface only when needed and does not slowly drain out and overflow the bearing when the machinery is at rest.

And one last intriguing detail was noticed: the possible evidence of the original, or at least very early, color scheme. The engine and tender are now painted an extremely dark green—Brunswick green—that is almost black. The boiler, springs, and other hardware are painted an ordinary gloss black. Nearly all wooden parts are Brunswick green. In the relatively dim light of the museum, most visitors assume the entire engine is painted black, but in the bright outside light the green-and-black color scheme became more evident. More interesting were traces of a much brighter green visible only in natural sunlight. After the engine came back to the museum, we made a more careful study and found the entire frame was once the lighter green. This paint is the first layer on the wood. It may be assumed that other wooden parts, such as the lagging, were painted in the same shade. The Munsell color number is 2.5G3/6.

The little *John Bull* revealed many secrets of her design and construction in the course of her 1980 rehabilitation and running. It was the running experience that was the most important; only after the first chuff of smoke from her stack and the first powered roll of her wheels did the major secrets come fully to light. We found an engine with suspension and axle rigging that were more advanced than anyone had suspected. We found not a crotchety or temperamental example of industrial antiquity but a machine that is wonderfully easy to operate. We gained a fresh appreciation of the profound creativity that early English and American engineers applied to the world's earliest railways. And we found, as did Steinbeck, that a live specimen is a far different thing than a lifeless one.[6]

Notes

1. William L. Withuhn, memo to *John Bull* record, 17 Mar. 1980. In "Report on the Mechanical and Safety Inspection of the *John Bull* by the Hartford Steam Boiler Inspection and Insurance Co., 11 March–13 March 1980," Smithsonian accessions.

2. Withuhn, memo dated 28 Mar. 1980: "Estimate of Performance of the *John Bull* at 40 psi, When Running with Tender or with Tender and C&A Coach No. 3," Smithsonian accessions. The formula used was Tractive Effort $= \dfrac{KPC^2S}{D}$, with cylinders $11'' \times 20''$, and $K = .8$. Horsepower $= \dfrac{T_v V}{375}$.

3. Withuhn, memo dated 25 Apr. 1980: "Estimate of Evaporative Demand, When Running the *John Bull* at 40 psi," Smithsonian accessions.

4. John Steinbeck, *The Log from the Sea of Cortez* (New York, 1941), p. 2.

5. *See* John H. White, Jr., "Introduction of the Locomotive Safety Truck," United States National Museum Bulletin 228, Contributions from the Museum of History and Technology, Paper 24 (Washington, D.C., 1961), pp. 129–31.

6. Another account of the 1980 test was published in *Railroad History* 144 (Spring 1981) and in *American Heritage*, Aug.–Sept. 1981.

Appendix B: Memo Specifications, 1830

Robert L. Stevens

Mr. Stevens' Engine
Liverpool Railway Office   Dec. 6th, 1830

Jones's Wheels if not found objectionable and 4 ft. 6 in. in diameter and wholly wrought iron.

The Boiler 2 ft. 6 in. diameter and 6 ft. long. The fire box a vertical cylinder of as great a diameter as convenient. The Plate in the smoke box to be as light as practicable. The cylinders 9 inches diameter and 20 inch stroke, not more than ⅜ thick. The passages to 6 × 1⅛. The exhausting port to be larger and to have a chamber close to the cylinder with a large pipe to free the piston from any pressure—say, 4 in. in diameter. The piston rods to be partly steeled and 1⅜ diameter. The back covers to the cylinders to be of boiler plate.

The joints in the working gear to have straps and keys, and the pin of the eye to be forged in. The guides to be of steel instead of pullies. The cranked axles to be 3¼ inches. The brasses to have more bearing sideways. The Boiler to be kept as low as possible.

The depth of the fire box to be 3 feet. The top of fire box to be braced up to the dome. The boiler to be scant ¼ inch thick but the vertical part to be a full ¼ inch. The chimmey [*sic*] to be a good size.

Four wheels to be alike and coupled on the outside. The side rods to be open work if it be found adviseable.

The cylinders placed to work underneath the angle next the cylinder, the same as the large Engine for Inclined Plane. The tubes to be made of iron as thin as possible. This engine to be completed and delivered in time for the March Packet, 1831.

R. Stephenson
Robt. L. Stevens

N.B. The crease of the wheels to be 1½ in. deep. The Rails are 5 feet from centre to centre and 2¼ in. broad. Inside breadth 4 ft. 9¾ in. To work expansively at ½ stroke.

Appendix C: Roster of Camden and Amboy Locomotives, 1831 to 1872

William D. Edson

Roster Notes

William D. Edson is a mechanical engineer with the Federal Railroad Administration whose avocation is compiling locomotive rosters. The present list is based on materials assembled by the Railway and Locomotive Historical Society that are now cared for by Mr. Edson. The basic data is from lists complied by the C&A Railroad in 1840, 1850, and 1867, together with data assembled by the late J. D. Lovell (d. 1947) of Hollidaysburg, Pennsylvania, a longtime employee of the Pennsylvania Railroad's Altoona shops. Lovell had access to early motive-power records once housed at Altoona. The 1885 memo of Isaac Dripps was the basis for information on the earliest C&A locomotives. Dimensions are in inches. Letters in parentheses refer to notes at the end of the roster.

Abbreviations used:
DR = dropped
RB = rebuilt
SC = scrapped
SO = sold

C&A Name & No.		Reno. 1/72	Type	Builder	C/N	Date	RB	Cylin.-Dr.-Weight	Disposition
		(PRR)							
John Bull	1	601	2-2-2-0 (b)	Steph.	25	6/31		9x20-54	Donated '85 (b)
	2		" (c)	Hob. shop		'33	'50	" "	DR by '53
	3		" "	"		"	'49	" "	" '59 (d)
	4		" "	"		6/33		" "	" "
	5		" "	E. K. Dod		'33	'49	" "	Wrecked '45 (d)
	6		" "	"		"		" "	DR by '53 (e)
	7		" "	"		"		" "	" '64 (d)
	8		" "	"		'34		" "	DR by '53
North America	9		" "	Hob. shop		'35	'49	" "	" '64 (e)
	10		" "	"		"	'50	" "	" " (f)
	11		" "	"		"		9-¾x20-54	" " (d)
	12		" "	"		'36		" "	" " (e)
	13		" "	"		"		" "	" " (d)
	14		" "	"		'37		" "	DR by '65 (d)
	15		" "	Dunham		"		13x20-54	" "
	16		" "	Borden. shops		"	(g)	" "	" "
Monster	17		0-8-0	"		'38?	(h)	18x27-48	RB '52 4-6-0 No. 35
(Ex-Phila. & Tren.)	18(i)		4-2-0	(Baldwin		?)	'48	10½x16-54	DR by '66
" "	19 "		"	("		?)	'49	"	" "
	20		4-2-0?	Newcastle		?	'45	10½x18	" "
Ben Franklin	21		4-4-0	Norris		12/45		14x22-60-45,400	DR by '58
E. A. Stevens	22		"	Baldwin	243	1/45	'55, '68	13-¾x18-60-41,700	SC 2/72
(Ex-Phila. & Tren.)	23(i)		4-2-0	(Baldwin	?	?)		10½x16	DR by '58
" "	24 "		"	("	?	?)	'47	" -54	" "
	25	625	4-4-0	Norris		1/48		14x22-69-47,300	SC 1/72 (j)
	26	626	"	"		2/48		" " "	SC 5/72 "
	27	627	"	Newcastle		'48	'69	14½x20-60-44,600	SC 3/72
John Stevens	28		6-2-0	Norris		5/49	(?)	13x34-84	DR by '68
	29		"	"		1/50		13x38-96-47,000	RB '55 2nd No. 29 (4-4-0)
	30		"	"	(k)	2/50		13½x38- " "	RB '56 " " 30 (4-4-0)

C&A Name & No.	Reno. 1/72	Type	Builder	C/N	Date	RB	Cylin.-Dr.-Weight	Disposition
31		"	"	(k)	c. '50		" " "	RB '57 " " 31 (4-4-0)
32		"	"		c. '50		" " "	RB '62 " " 32 (4-4-0)
33		0-8-0 (1)	Trenton		'52		18x30-48-66,405	SC by '72
34		" "	"		"		" " "	RB '69 to 2nd No. 34
35	635	" "	Borden. shop		"		" " "	SC 2/74
36	636	4-4-0	Norris		'53		14x24-54-51,600	SO 11/74 S. C. Glading
37	—	6-2-0	"		4/53	(m)	13½x38-84	RB '56 2nd No. 37 (4-4-0)
38	—	"	"		"	"	14x38-84	RB '53 2nd No. 38 (4-4-0)
39	639 (n)	4-4-0	"		"	8/70	14x24-54-52,500	SO 9/86 A. H. King
40	640 (o)	"	D. Cooke		"		15x20-66-53,850	
41	641	"	Rogers	399	6/53		" " - 65,000	SC 3/80
42	642	0-8-0 (1)	Trenton		'54	(p)	18x30-48-70,000	SO 7/74 S. C. Glading
43	—	" "	"		"	(q)	" " "	SC by '71
44	644	4-4-0	D. Cooke		'53		15x20-66-52,450	SC 4/72
45	645	" —	Baldwin	570	1/54		15x22-60-53,475	SC 1/78
46	646	"	Norris		'53	'70	" " -55,920	SO 10/74 S. C. Glading
47	647	"	N. Jer. L&M		'52		16x20-60-55,600	SO 7/79 E. H. Wilson
48	648	"	Rogers	541	10/54		15½x20-66-55,750	SC 5/78
49	649	"	"	544	11/54		" " "	SC 2/75
50	650	"	"	548	11/54		" " "	SC 4/77
51	651	"	"	551	12/54		" " "	SC 4/72
52	652 reF&JA No. 3 No. 266 (r)	"	Trenton		'55	'69	15½x24-72-61,450	SO 6/81 E. H. Wilson
53	653	"	Norris		'53		15x22-72-59,650	SC 10/72
54	654	"	"		"		" " "	SC 3/73

C&A Name & No.		Réno. 1/72	Type	Builder	C/N	Date	RB	Cylin.-Dr.-Weight	Disposition
	55	655	"	"		"		" " "	SC 2/73
	56	656	"	"		"	'70	15x22-60-55,920	SC 5/78
	57	657	"	"		"	'71	" " "	SC 4/74
Crampton Conversions 1853–62									
(2nd)	38	638	4-4-0	RB from	6-2-0	'53	(s)	13x38-72-62,680	SC 6/72
"	29	629	"	"	"	'55		" "-59,000	SC 4/74
"	30	630	"	"	"	'56	(k)	13½x38-72-59,320	SC 4/74
"	37	637	"	"	"	"		" "-59,750	SO 7/74 S. C. Glading
"	31	631	"	"	"	'57	(k)	" "-59,320	SC 4/74
"	32	632	"	"	"	'62		" "-61,390	SC 4/74
Replacements 1858–59									
(2nd)	21	621	4-4-0	D. Cooke		'58		13x22-60-49,500	SC 11/81
"	23	623	"	"		"		14x24-66-55,655	SC 4/79 CPR 284?
"	24	624	"	"		"		" " "	SO 9/74 S. C. Glading
"	2	602	"	"		'59		14½x24-66-55,450	SC 4/76
"	3	603	"	"		"		" " "	"
"	4	604	"	"		"		" " "	"
"	5	605	"	"		"		" " "	SO 3/81 J. H. Brakeley
New Additions 1860–63									
	58	658	4-4-0	C&A shop		'60		14x26-66-54,000	SC 2/75
	59	659	"	N. Jer. L&M		'61		16x24-60-59,350	SO 5/79 Wm. Collier
	60	660	"	D. Cooke		'61		" -54-58,617	SO 5/78 " "
	61	661 (re6/82) B-D 3019	"	"		"	'71	" "-58,380	DR c. '87
	62	662	"	Rogers	1001	5/61		16x24-54-60,905	SC 3/72
	63	663	"	C&A shop		'62	(t)	14½x26-66-57,230	SO 12/85 E. H. Wilson
	64	664	"	D. Cooke		'62		16x24-60-59,680	SC 6/73

C&A Name & No.		Reno. 1/72	Type	Builder	C/N	Date	RB	Cylin.-Dr.-Weight	Disposition
	65	665	"	"		"		" " "	SO 4/82 E. H. Wilson
	66	666	"	"		"		" "-58,230	SO 3/86 "
	67	667	"	"		"		" " "	SO 3/81 "
	68	668	"	"		"		" "-60,705	SC 11/72
	69	669	"	"		"		" " "	SC 3/74
	70	670	"	C&A shop		'62	(t)	14½x26-66-59,450	SC 5/78
	71	671	"	D. Cooke		'63		16x24-60-58,625	SO 7/84 E. H. Wilson
	72	672	"	"		"—		" " "	SO 12/85
	73	673	"	"		"		" "-59,730	SC 4/79
	74	674	"	"		"		" " "	DR '74
	(re 1/74 W.Jer. 5								
Replacements 1864–69									
(2nd)	6	606	4-4-0	C&A shop		'64		14x26-66-58,680	SC 1/75
"	7	607	"	" "		"		" " "	SC 1/76
"	8	608	"	" "		'65		" " "	SC 1/76
"	9	609	"	" "		"	(t)	" "-59,250	SO 10/81 E. H. Wilson
"	10	610	"	" "		"	"	" " "	SO 7/79 C&MR (u)
"	11	611	"	" "		"	"	" " "	SO 4/81 Wm. Collier
"	12	612	"	D. Cooke		'64		16x24-60-60,980	SO 4/81 J. H. Brakeley
"	13	613	"	" "		"		" " "	SO 5/75 R.&D. (v)
"	14	614	"	" "		'65		16x24-54-59,005	SO 1/89 E. H. Wilson
"	15	615	"	" "		"		" " "	SO 1/89 E. H. Wilson
"	16	616	"	" "		"		" " "	SO 11/90 "
"	17	617	"	" "		"		" " "	DR c. '92
	re F&JA No. 1, No. 119 (w)								
"	18	618	"	C&A shop		'66		15x26-66-59,450	SO 4/81 Wm. Collier
"	19	619	"	" "		"		" " "	SO 9/78 "
"	20	620	"	" "		?	(x)	13x20-54-36,650	SC 4/77

C&A Name & No.		Reno. 1/72	Type	Builder		C/N	Date	RB	Cylin.-Dr.-Weight	Disposition
"	28	628	"	"	"		'68		16x22-60-57,840	SC 5/78
"	34	634	4-6-0	"	"		4/69		17x24-54-71,100	SO 10/79 E. H. Wilson
New Additions 1866—72										
	75	675	4-4-0	"	"		'66		15x28-60-60,580	SO 1/90 E. H. Wilson
	76	676	"	"	"		"		" " "	SC 4/79
	77	677	2-6-0	"	"		'67		17x24-54-71,150	SO 10/79 E. H. Wilson
	78	678	"	"	"		"		" " "	" "
	79	679 (re 6/82) B-D 3020	"	"	"		"		" " "	DR c. '89
	81	681	4-4-0	"	"		'68		16x24-66-65,100	SO 10/91 E. H. Wilson
	82	682	"	"	"		6/68		" "-64,100	" "
	83	683 (re 8/89) Union Tr. Co. No. 1	"	"	"		12/68		" "-65,000	
	84	684 (re 8/88) Union Tr. Co.	"	"	"		'69		" "-65,100	
	85	685	2-6-0	"	"		4/69		17x24-54-71,150	SO 4/89 E. H. Wilson
	86	686	4-4-0	"	"		'69		17x24-60-68,500	SO 6/86 Std. Coal Co.
	87	687	"	"	"		8/69		" " "	SC 3/80
	88	688	"	"	"		'69		" " "	SC 4/80
	89	689	"	"	"		"		16x24-66-70,400	SO 6/86 E. H. Wilson
	90	690	"	"	"		3/70		" " "	SC 12/94
	91	691	"	"	"		4/70		" " "	SO 8/87 E. H. Wilson
	92	692 (re 6/91) Union Tr. Co. No. 1	"	"	"		6/70		" " "	
	93	693	"	"	"		'70		17x24-60-69,700	SO 12/93 E. H. Wilson
	94	694	"	"	"		10/70		" "-69,800	" "
	95	695	"	"	"		12/70		" "-69,600	SO 10/80 "
	96	696	"	"	"		2/71		" " "	SO 12/93

C&A Name & No.		Reno. 1/72	Type	Builder	C/N	Date	RB	Cylin.-Dr.-Weight	Disposition
		re U.T. No. 1, 683 (y)							
	97	697	"	" "		4/71		" "-68,500	SO 8/86 "
	98	698	"	" "		6/71		" "-67,500	SO 12/93 "
	(99)	699	"	" "		1/72		17x24-66-70,800	SC 12/94
	(100)	700	"	" "		4/72		" "-69,300	"
Additional C&A Locomotives of Uncertain Origin									
	A	764	4-4-0	C&A shop		'66		13x20-54-44,400	SO 3/86 E. H. Wilson
	B	765	"	" "		"		" " "	SO 4/81 Wm. Collier
	C	766	"	" "		"		" " "	SO 10/74 P. S. Ross
	D	767	"	" "		"		" " "	SO 6/88 Hampton Coal
	E	768	"	D. Cooke		4/57		13x20-60-47,200	SC 7/78
	F	769	"	" .		'56		13x22-66-48,950	SO 4/79 Wm. Collier
	G	770	0-4-0	"		8/56		11x20-40-45,700	SO 3/86 E. H. Wilson

Possibly these were acquired in 1868 when the C&A leased the Camden & Burlington County (4 locos.); Vincentown Branch (1 loco.); and Pemberton & Hightstown (3 locos.).

A dozen additional C&A locomotives are listed by Lovell. They were delivered just before the lease became effective, some of them without any lettering:

152-156 re PRR 752-756 2-6-0 BLW. 8&9/71 17x24-54-71,150

157-161 " " 757-761 " D. Cooke 9-11/71 " " "

162-163 " " 762-763 4-4-0 C&A shop No. 8,10/71 17x24-66-70,800

Note a—Weights for engines in service in 1867 are listed as shown in the C&A roster for that year. Weights for engines built after 1867 are listed as shown by Lovell after being acquired by PRR.

b—The *John Bull* was built as 0-4-0 with 9x20 cylinders. It was soon rebuilt as a 2-2-2-0 with a two-wheel pilot truck and 11½x20 cylinders. Weight was 24,625 lbs. in 1867 (see text).

c—Nos. 2-16 were apparently built as 2-2-2-0.

d—Nos. 3,5,7,11,13, and 14 were rebuilt with 11½x20 cylinders.

e—Nos. 6,9, and 12 were rebuilt with 13x20 cylinders; No. 8 with 11x16.

f—No. 10 listed as 4-4-0 in R&LHS Bulletin 101. Cylinders 13x20. Must be as rebuilt.

g—No. 16 built by C&A at Bordentown according to Lovell and Dripps.

h—No. 17 date of completion is uncertain. Lovell claims it was rebuilt as No. 35 in 1852. James White claimed the No. 17 was retired in the early 1860s and was not rebuilt.

i—Nos. 18,19,23,24 probably acquired with Philadelphia & Trenton, operated by C&A effective 1836. P&T engines included *Trenton* (Baldwin c/n 5 10/34), *Blackhawk* (BLW. 11 5/35), *Pennsylvania* (B. 45 8/36), and *New Jersey* (BLW. 58 11/36). A fifth engine, *Philadelphia* (BLW. 165 '39), is listed in R&LHS Bulletin 101.

j—No. 625 listed by Lovell with 66" drivers, and No. 626 with 60".

k—Date rebuilt as 4-4-0 in question. Drawings made in 1860 and 1862 show the Nos. 30 and 31 as 6-2-

O's. See Chapter II.

l—Nos. 33,34,35,42, and 43 were rebuilt from 0-8-0 *Monster* types to 4-6-0.

m—Nos. 37 and 38 specs. were 14x38-96-47,000 according to another source.

n—No. 639 Reno. 2/73 to Freehold & Jamesburg Agricultural No. 2, then RE 9/79 PRR No. 257.

o—No. 640 Reno. 3/74 to F&JA No. 1 (?).

p—No. 642 listed by Lovell as 18x29-44-70,450. Roster of 1867 shows 18x30-66-70,000.

q—No. 43 listed by Lovell as 4-4-0, 18x30-66. Roster of 1867 shows 18x30-66-70,000.

r—No. 652 Reno. 6/73 to F&JA No. 3, Reno. 9/79 PRR No. 266. Specs. as RB: 16x24-60-65,000.

s—No. 638 listed by Lovell with 14x38 cylinders.

t—Nos. 663, 670, 609, 610, and 611 listed by Lovell with 15x26 cylinders.

u—No. 610 sold to Cumberland & Maurice River Railroad.

v—No. 613 sold to Richmond & Danville Railroad, probably their No. 52.

w—No. 617 Reno. 1/76 to F&JA No. 1, then Reno. 9/79 to PRR No. 119.

x—No. 620 listed by Lovell with 14x24 cylinders, 60″ drivers.

y—No. 696 Reno. 8/88 to Union Transportation Co. No. 1, then Reno. 8/89 to PRR No. 683.

Dispositions: Glading, Wilson, and Collier were all apparently secondhand equipment dealers.

Appendix D: Running Regulations for the Camden and Amboy Railroad, ca. 1855

ARTICLE I.—Each Conductor, Engine Driver, Switch Tender and Bridge Tender, will be supplied with a good watch by the Company.

ARTICLE II.—The CONDUCTOR will call for and receive two Watches at the office, preceding each departure—compare them with the Standard Clock, and be sure they agree before leaving the room—hand one to the ENGINE DRIVER to run by—receive it from him again at the end of his route, and return both to the office as soon as he arrives. Compare his time with the Clocks at the Stations he stops at, and notify the Agents of any discrepancy. Know that the Bell Rope is in order and properly attached, and that the Brakemen are in their places, before starting the Train.

ARTICLE III.—The fastest rate of running permitted with Through Trains, is one mile in 1½ minutes, and with Way and Accommodation Trains one mile in 2 minutes (when behind time) and on straight track only. On the Sharp Curves near Amboy, Crosswicks Creek Bridge and Embankment, the Curve at the Aquaduct, over the Delaware Bridge, while passing the Shops at Bordentown, and any Way Station reduce the speed one-half. Never run through Towns or Villages faster than permitted by the Authorities thereof—approach and pass all Turnouts and Stations with the greatest caution and watchfulness.

ARTICLE IV.—CONDUCTORS have charge of their respective trains, and all employed therewith, while on the route; and will be held responsible for the violation of any of the requirements contained in the Time Table or Running Regulations, by any person employed on the train or road, as sanctioning such violation, unless they shall, before the next passage, report in writing on their time list.

ARTICLE V.—The CONDUCTOR shall pass through all the passenger cars between each Station, when the train stops.

ARTICLE VI.—The Baggage Master, while the train is in motion, shall attend the Second Brake from the Engine.

ARTICLE VII.—CONDUCTORS and ENGINE DRIVERS will at all times while running, be provided with the time tables of the road, and *allow no person,* other than the *fireman* attached, to ride on the *Engine or Tender,* without an order from a proper agent.

ARTICLE VIII.—BRAKEMEN shall always be in their places, when the train starts, (one in the gig-top on the tender, another on the front platform of the last passenger car,) and not leave them, while the train is in motion; they shall watch the train constantly, and be prepared to give and obey the signals promptly.

ARTICLE IX.—ENGINE DRIVERS shall always approach a *Draw Bridge* so slowly that they can under any circumstances stop short of it; and never attempt to cross, without coming to a full stop, unless they see a white flag exhibited in the hands of the Bridge Tender by day, or a yellow light at night.—If the signals are properly shown and seen, they may pass without stopping, but shall not proceed at a rate faster than a man can walk, until the Engine has passed the draw.

ARTICLE X.—Each Draw Bridge Tender shall be at the draw at the passing of each Train, and when the draw is right, and securely fastened, hold up a white flag by day, or a yellow light by night; and he shall not open the draw, or remove the fastenings, after hearing the whistle, or seeing an approaching Train, till it has passed.

ARTICLE XI.—Whenever any Train or Engine has passed on or off of a Turnout, the Switch Bars must be immediately set and secured for the Main Track by the Switch Tender, or in his absence, the Conductor, if there is one, and if not, the Engine Driver is required to know that it is done.

ARTICLE XII.—The Switches are to be exclusively under the control of the Switch Tender, and he shall not suffer any one to interfere or meddle with them in any manner.

ARTICLE XIII.—The wedges and locks and bolts of no Switch shall be moved, or the Switch opened, when any train is due or expected, and no Gravel, Freight or Subordinate Train shall be let off from a branch or side track, until the Train due, or having the right of the track, has passed; and the Switch Tender is responsible for the Switch being in the right position for the Trains, and any neglect of duty or violation of orders, will cause his immediate discharge.

ARTICLE XIV.—Every Switch Tender must see, that the Turnouts are kept clear at the Stations, where Trains are liable to meet, and that no Cars or other obstructions are permitted to interfere with the passing Trains, and the Switch Tender, who is absent from his duty, without the consent of the Superintendent, shall be forthwith discharged.

ARTICLE XV.—If the Train fails to arrive at New Brunswick, Princeton or Trenton, fifteen minutes after it is due at either of said Stations, it shall be the duty of the Agent at such Station to Telegraph to the Stations towards which, the Train is going, of the non-arrival of the Train, and also when the Train leaves.

ARTICLE XVI.—If a regular Through Passenger Train should fail for one hour, to arrive at any Station, where there is an extra Engine, the person having charge of the Station, shall send an Engine in pursuit of the missing train, with orders to proceed with great caution.

ARTICLE XVII.—If a regular Through Passenger Train cannot arrive at a Locomotive Station, until one hour after its regular time, it must expect a Relief Engine to start from the Locomotive Station, and must proceed with great caution, after the time when it would cross, or meet the Relief Engine, going at the ordinary speed.

ARTICLE XVIII.—No person in the service of the Company, while on duty, connected wtih any of the Trains, will be permitted either to smoke or use ardent spirits, and if any such person shall be at all under its influence while on duty, he shall be dismissed.

ARTICLE XIX.—ENGINE DRIVERS with regular trains may run with confidence to the various places *up to the time specified in the time table* and as provided for by regulations for opposing Trains to leave, then if they do not meet, proceed with the utmost caution until seen by each other, when the one farthest from the meeting post will go immediately back to the turn out, and pass with the least possible delay to either train.

ARTICLE XX.—All Regular Freight Trains will keep out of the way of all Regular Passenger Trains, both Way and Through, and wait on Turnouts until they have passed, or have been heard from and received permission from the Conductor of the Passenger Train to proceed.

ARTICLE XXI.—All Extra Trains and Engines will keep out of the way of all Regular Trains, both Passenger and Freight, and never approach a Station where one is expected, unless it can arrive on the Turnout at least 10 minutes before the Regular Train is due; and Engine Drivers must, at all times, and under all circumstances, (making due allowance for the worst condition of the track) pass over the road with sufficient caution and watchfulness to avoid a collision; looking constantly for opposing Trains, Engines, Hand cars and men repairing road, and come to a full stop at the regular stations. At night, or during the day send a man a-head with a signal, where they cannot see, or be seen from an opposing engine sufficiently far to stop with certainty without accident. Extra Engines with Freight Trains, are not to exceed a speed of one mile in 5 minutes, and without trains 1 mile in 3 minutes on any part of the road.

ARTICLE XXII.—Engine Drivers with Freight Trains are required to run between the Stations in the given time, at as nearly a uniform speed as possible, not to pass an Engine or Train faster than Five miles an hour.

ARTICLE XXIII.—The Conductor of each Train will provide himself with the latest time-tables of the road, and a watch to run by—he will see that a Red Light is exhibited on the last car of the Train at night, and that, on Trains drawn by the connected Coal Engines, there is a Brakeman stationed at every intervening 10 cars at the starting of his Train.

SIGNALS

Give a prolonged sound of the *whistle half a mile from each Station, Draw Bridge,* and 300 yards from *each road crossing,* as the Train approaches; *have the bell rung when passing through streets* and 300 yards from all *public roads* and continue until past.

One Tap of the Bell
signifies Go a-head

Give 1 short sound of the Whistle to loose the Brakes.

Two Taps of the Bell
signifies Stop.

Give 2 short sounds to apply the Brakes

Three Taps of the Bell
signifies go Back.

Give 3 short sounds to go Back.

A Red Flag by day, or a Red Light by night, signifies—Stop the Train. A White Flag by day, and a Yellow Light by night signifies—All is Right. If the signal of the White Flag by day and a Yellow Light by night, indicating that All is Right, is not distinctly seen by the Engine Driver at the Switches and Draw Bridges, he shall stop and ascertain that all is right before he proceeds.

All Signals must be withdrawn immediately after the train, for which it was exhibited, has passed.

Any absence of, or improper use of signals, must be immediately reported by the Engine Driver, to the Conductor, and by the Conductor to the Agent at the end of his route.

A True Copy from the Minutes of the Executive Committee.

J. S. GREEN, Secretary.

503476